All About Growing
Fruits &
Berries

Edited by
Will Kirkman

Designed by
Craig Bergquist

Photography by
William Aplin
Clyde Childress
Michael Landis
William Reasons

Illustrations by
Leavitt Dudley
Ron Hildebrand

Contents

What this book is all about

**Let your garden do more for you.
Plant fruit in the living-space portion using ideas and
answers from the pages that follow to help you
blend it into your landscape.**

That old equation, Fruit Tree=Orchard hangs on, even in
the minds of the most up-to-date gardeners, but it's
just not valid.

Fruiting plants these days come in such a range of sizes
and kinds that you can use them anywhere, from containers
on the terrace to hedges, ground cover, or shade trees.
Let us help you plan a fruit garden with the ideas included
here. We discuss landscape uses of fruit, container care,
dwarf trees, and varieties to suit your climate. Then we
list kinds of fruit, following page 20, and finally we discuss
care and training, following page 74.

As a quick example of how fruit can and should be used
in a landscaped garden, here's a little story.

While planning this book, we went to talk to one of the
most experienced and imaginative gardeners we know.
After talking a while he paused, thinking of the subject in
terms of his own garden. Then he said, "I guess I don't
have much fruit here."

The fact is, he does have fruit—everywhere on his
suburban lot. But it fits in so well that he'd forgotten it.
We took him on a mental tour of his own place.

"You have the persimmon, the pomegranate, and the
fig beside the driveway. And your two dwarf apple espaliers
behind the zinnias."

"Oh, yes," he said, "I do have some trees in front."

"Then you have the quince in the sideyard, a dwarf
mandarin, and the espaliered lemon and Rangpur lime
outside the bedroom."

"That's right," he said. "I've got quite a bit of fruit."

"You've got some in back, too," we went on. "The
kumquat, and the Japanese plum—in fact, this garden
is really an orchard."

Forgetting 11 fruit trees on a 50-foot lot may seem like
an extreme case of absent-mindedness, but this man's
trees fit right into the landscape, and take no more care
than his shrubs and a lot less than his annuals or his lawn.
He enjoys the spring flowers, picks ripe fruit in most
seasons, does a bit of spraying and pruning along with
his other garden chores, and never thinks of his town
orchard as special.

◁

*Top: This elegant row of espaliered apple trees in full leaf
makes a striking hedge.
Far left: 'Bonanza,' genetic dwarf peach, provides a big harvest.
Left: A trained dwarf apple tree planted in a box is a perfect
addition to a deck or terrace.*

Fruit plants are different now

Even years ago a gardener might put an apple tree in the
center of his lawn, or grow grapes over the summerhouse,
but until fairly recently a single fruit tree took up a great
deal of space and created so much shade that low-growing
fruit plants beneath it couldn't get enough sun for a crop.
All that has changed. Modern techniques of dwarfing and
simplified methods of training let you grow a dozen apple
varieties in the same garden and still have plenty of
sunny garden space for peaches, strawberries, and a
row of petunias.

We show you pictures on the following pages of a
garden that is only 15 feet by 50 feet and still holds 17 fruit
trees, several grape varieties, cane berries, and vegetables. And in the photographs opposite this page you
can see three distinct ways of planting fruit in small
spaces, all of which add to the beauty of the landscape:
You can train plants as hedges and espaliers (we discuss
techniques following page 78); you can buy genetic dwarf
plants like the little peach opposite; or you can combine
dwarf plants, training, and container gardening for an
orchard right on the terrace.

Using this book to plan your garden

The focus throughout this book is small-space gardening.
We draw from the work of plant scientists on dwarfing
rootstocks and genetic or natural dwarfs; from old and new
techniques of pruning and training that confine plants;
and from the experience of home gardeners willing to try
something new in landscape mixtures or container planting.

Start with the idea that anything is possible. Perhaps
you have a large deck with a few pots of annuals and
succulents on it, but you want fruit. Look at the container
discussion following page 8 for ideas on planting and care
of container trees. Read on into the discussion of dwarf
trees immediately following. Then choose your fruit from
the variety lists: perhaps a couple of apples, a peach, a
nectarine, some strawberries, and a grape vine.

You'll want the apples small, so choose a nursery,
either near you or from our catalog list, that can supply
full dwarf trees on Malling 9 or Malling 26 roots (or the
new Malling 27 when it's available). See the chart on
page 13. Among peaches and nectarines, the new genetic
dwarfs have abundant double flowers and attractive leaves
and are just right in a container. Your strawberries can
go into a special jar or barrel, your grapes into a trellis
container. Look at the final section of the book for dis-
cussions of planting, container soil, pruning, and training,
then set out your plants and enjoy them.

Fruit in the landscape

When you landscape with fruit plants, you combine beauty with down-to-earth practicality. On these pages we show a charming garden entirely devoted to fruit plants, more than 20 kinds, all growing in a space just 15 feet by 50. We'll discuss this garden in detail, but first we'd like to outline some of the many possibilities for working fruit plants into a more usual landscape. We'll break our suggestions down by the standard landscape categories.

Trees for shade or for ornament

For shade over an outdoor sitting area, use standard-sized apples or large crabapples, pruning them to branch high, or try a spreading cherry such as 'Napoleon' ('Royal Ann').

For a medium-sized lawn tree for shade and ornament, use an apple on semidwarf roots (MM 106), or an apricot if climate permits.

Good ornamental trees for the middle distance include showy-flowered peaches, semidwarf cherries, figs, the larger crabapples, and citrus.

For an especially striking effect in mild climates use a persimmon for its fall color and winter fruit, or a pomegranate for its big orange flowers and globes of red fruit.

Shrubs and hedge plants

Genetic dwarf peaches make splendid flowering hedges with abundant spring bloom and ornamental fruit among the leaves. Train showy-flowered semidwarf or standard peaches the same way.

Apples and pears on Malling 9, 26, or 7 roots can be trained to an informal hedge against trellis or fence, and as formal espaliers. See page 78.

For shrub borders try the smallest crabapples, blueberries, or currants. The last are especially rewarding, with ornamental flowers and clusters of scarlet fruit. Or try edible ornamentals such as chokecherry, cornelian-cherry (*Cornus mas*), Oregon grape, pyracantha, *Viburnum trilobum* (high-bush cranberry), or elderberry.

Ground covers

For small areas of ground cover, use fruiting strawberry, but plan to replace it every three years with new plants if you want a heavy crop. For larger areas use cranberry, low-bush blueberry, or some of the low and spreading pyracanthas and mahonias.

Especially striking flowers or fruit

Among temperate region fruit trees, the most striking in bloom are apples, crabapples, showy-flowered peaches, cherries, and quince.

Among tender crops, citrus offers the best perfume, and there are beautiful flowers on pineapple guava and passionvine.

For showy fruit, crabapple is the hardiest and most striking. In mild climates, persimmons and pomegranates are good, and citrus is showy over a long season.

Among edible ornamentals the best effect of all comes from mountain-ash *(Sorbus)*, bearing huge clusters of scarlet berries on a small tree.

Big fruit garden, 15 by 50

The garden shown in our photographs belongs to David Whiting of St. Helena, California. You may not want a

Top, Whiting garden looking north at entrance. Bottom, looking south, where one variety of nectarine, and multiple varieties of raspberries, currants, grapes, berries, and pears are planted.

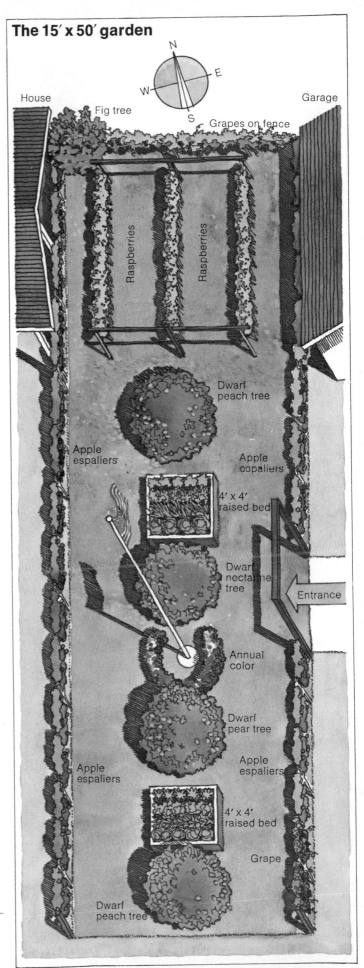

The 15′ x 50′ garden

House
Fig tree
Garage
Grapes on fence
Raspberries
Raspberries
Dwarf peach tree
Apple espaliers
Apple espaliers
4′ x 4′ raised bed
Dwarf nectarine tree
Entrance
Annual color
Dwarf pear tree
Apple espaliers
Apple espaliers
4′ x 4′ raised bed
Grape
Dwarf peach tree

garden of only fruiting plants, but you can borrow Mr. Whiting's techniques, even if fruit will form only part of your landscape.

The important basics

Look over the plan on page 5 and notice first the orientation of the garden. The sun, in passing from east to west, lights both sides of all the plants. Fruit needs sun to set a crop. You should always plan to have fruit plants exposed to the south or west sun if you can't manage the all-day exposure of this garden.

Examine, too, the training of these plants. Dwarf apples and pears on open trellises form an attractive hedge, and the training exposes the branches to a maximum of light for heavy crops. Cane berries are also trellised and oriented approximately north and south. They take little space and bear heavily. In the center of the garden a pruned dwarf pear and genetic dwarf peaches and nectarines act as decorative shrubs, offering bloom and fruit. Grapes are mainly planted on the north side of the garden with full southern exposure to develop good sugar in the fruit. Raised beds produce vegetables in this garden, but could also be planted with small fruits or annuals for cut flowers and color.

If you choose to combine fruiting plants with more standard ornamentals, one of many possible variations on this garden might be to plant an apple or pear hedge as shown on the entrance side, backed by a lawn. A paved sitting area where Mr. Whiting grows berries could hold a few genetic dwarf peaches or nectarines in containers, and perhaps a few strawberry barrels.

At the rear, among ornamental shrubs, you could use a fruiting crabapple for its spring bloom and decorative edible fruit.

Efficient training cuts your work

Fruit plants need maintenance if you hope for crops, but you don't want to spend your life as an apple babysitter. Mr. Whiting's training takes an initial effort, but once plants are established this way they get good light, perfect air circulation and plenty of rootspace, so they need the least possible babying with sprays, fertilizers, and shears. On page 84 we tell you how to do formal espaliers like those on the Whiting trellises, but we also suggest a method that takes less time at the start. You bend young trees at an angle, then trim all new growth to stubs with four leaves each. In a couple of seasons you have a handsome fruit hedge.

Trained dwarf plants make maintenance a lot easier since you can reach every part of them. The necessary sprays for pests or diseases go on in minutes when the distance from root to branch tip is only four or five feet. Pruning is quicker too, for a couple of reasons. First, you practice summer pruning. An occasional nip with the shears during the warm months means that winter pruning is almost entirely finished before winter; whatever branches you missed on your ordinary garden inspections are down where you can reach them. No ladders or pole pruners are necessary.

Even feeding and watering are easier with trained dwarf plants. The roots are shallow, so you don't need deep watering basins and hours of soaking. And since you want controlled growth, you apply less fertilizer and save money.

◁

Top: Looking north, the Whiting garden as it looked in spring. Spray emitters in raised beds maintain even moisture.
Bottom: In mid-summer, crops in raised beds have grown to provide vegetables along with the ripening fruit.

David Whiting harvests fruit from one of three different peach trees in his garden.

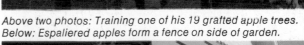

Above two photos: Training one of his 19 grafted apple trees. Below: Espaliered apples form a fence on side of garden.

Containers with fruit

At Versailles in the 1600's, Louis XIV's gardeners grew orange trees in pots. In summer they lined the walks of the palace gardens, then wheeled the trees indoors to the orangerie, a special greenhouse, when snow fell. Some of the trees are said to have lasted 75 years.

The general techniques of caring for a container orchard really haven't changed much in the last few hundred years, but modern dwarfing techniques cut the work of caring for container trees considerably, since dwarf trees are far less likely to get rootbound and cause problems with watering and feeding.

Following page 12 we discuss dwarf trees in detail, both grafted and natural, but first we'll outline the step-by-step techniques of planting and care that will keep your portable orchard healthy and productive for years.

Climate and container trees

The historical anecdote above gives you one good reason for planting in containers. Even tender plants far from their natural climate zone will grow well, since you can move them to shelter when cold weather comes (or wheel them to a shady spot if desert heat is your problem).

With containers, there's no reason not to try 'Meyer' lemons in Michigan or peaches in North Dakota. Your winter holding site should have plenty of light, but not too much heat, and you'll have to be careful not to overwater while the plants are inactive. Citrus is decorative enough to come into the house and fill a south window, but deciduous material can probably survive a season in the garage if you get it into the sun on fine spring days.

One warning: just because a plant can survive winter in the ground where you live doesn't mean it can manage cold weather in a container. If your garden soil freezes, then container soil will also freeze, killing your plants. Gardeners in the coldest northern zones should plan to protect even hardy deciduous plants in the coldest months.

What plants to choose

Our variety lists and the pages on dwarf trees will give you more extensive information on plants that suit containers. Here are just a few ideas to guide you: apples on Malling 9, 26, or 7 rootstocks; pears on quince roots; genetic dwarf peaches, nectarines, apricot, or cherry; any fig; the smaller crabapples; citrus on trifoliate orange roots where available; strawberries; spur-pruned grape varieties. When the new Malling 27 rootstock becomes widely available for apples, it should be ideal for container planting.

Size of container

Begin your container orchard with containers that are just 2 or 3 inches wider than the roots of your plants. If you start with a bareroot apple or pear, or one of the genetic dwarf fruits, your first container will be about the size of a 5-gallon lard can. In fact, since it will only be in use for one growing season, you might use a lard can and cover it with a basket or box. Let the young tree grow for a season and fill the container with roots, then repot it the following spring.

Evergreen fruit plants such as citrus should start their lives in a container that's not too much bigger than their rootball. If your soil mix is well drained you can go to a box 3 or 4 inches wider than the roots all around. For large nursery plants, the first container may be the permanent container.

Grapes in containers (Muscat above, 'Kings Ruby' below) take frequent attention to water and feeding, but look good. Supply a trellis for training.

Espaliered 'Gravenstein' apple is pretty and sets a good crop.

Breakfast comes fresh from your own 'Sequoia' strawberry "tree."

The maximum for permanent containers should be about bushel-basket size. Anything bigger will be too bulky to handle or move. (But consider a platform on wheels for any large container.) Half barrels are about the right size, or any box or pot that holds about that volume of soil. The minimum permanent size should be about 18 inches on a side and 18 inches deep. The smaller the container, the more work is involved in feeding, watering, and root pruning.

Any container is more practical if it can be taken apart. One side can be attached with screws, or better yet, all four sides can be screwed together for easy removal. The reason: container trees must be removed from their pots every two or three years for root pruning as described in the sketches on pages 10 and 11. Otherwise all the feeder roots bunch at the walls of the container and the plant languishes.

Move plants from the first, 5-gallon size container to the bushel size over two or three seasons. The right size of container lets the plant find water and nutrients easily, keeps soil from going sour around and beneath the roots, and slows top growth.

Container soil mix

We discuss synthetic soils on page 107. Some gardeners like to add a little rich loam to the mix of sand and organic material. It holds water better and helps keep nutrients available. Add up to one-third loam if you like, but be careful not to include clay soil. It holds water too well for a container mix, and you may drown your plants. For a purely synthetic mix, you'll have to be careful about feeding. The nutrients you add leach away when you water. Keep to a regular schedule as outlined below.

Feeding container fruit

Use the growth of the plant and its general appearance as your main guides to feeding. It should leaf out and grow vigorously in the spring and early summer, and leaves should be a healthy medium green. Yellowed leaves suggest a lack of nitrogen, while very dark leaves may mean you're feeding too much.

One method is to give each plant about half the recommended quantity of complete fertilizer (containing nitrogen, phosphoric acid, and potassium or potash) about every two to three weeks. A liquid fertilizer is easy to handle and less likely to burn roots. If the container says 1 tablespoon per gallon of water, use 1½ teaspoons instead.

Another good method is to use one of the pelleted slow-release fertilizers. These dissolve slowly over a period of time so you won't wash them away in the first week or so.

Feed through the growing season if the plant is to receive winter protection. Stop about mid-July if it is to stay outdoors. That will give it a chance to harden up new growth.

A note of caution: Fertilizer can build up in a pot when the drainage is poor and begin to burn the plant. You'll probably see brown, dry-looking leaf edges first. If you do, water heavily as described in the section below on watering. This heavy watering, or leaching, will clean the soil.

Citrus requires about the same amount of feeding as deciduous fruit, but it may also require a few extra nutrients. Special citrus foods containing iron, zinc, and sometimes other minerals are available at nurseries. Use them regularly, or switch to them if you see leaves with yellowed portions between bright green veins. If the leaf is uniformly yellow, veins and all, the plant lacks nitrogen. Citrus food won't hurt deciduous plants if you want to use it—but it may cost more.

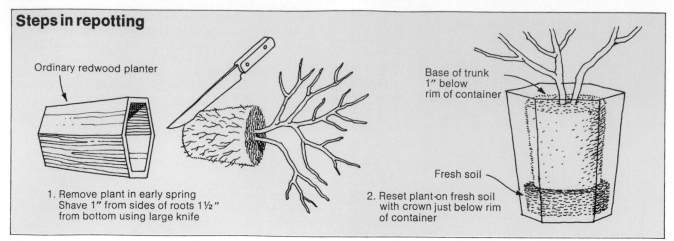

Steps in repotting

Ordinary redwood planter

Base of trunk
1″ below
rim of container

Fresh soil

1. Remove plant in early spring
Shave 1″ from sides of roots 1½″
from bottom using large knife

2. Reset plant on fresh soil
with crown just below rim
of container

Watering containers

Again, judge watering by the behavior of your plant. It should never wilt, but it shouldn't stand in soggy soil either. If you check the soil occasionally by digging down an inch or two, you'll soon learn how much to water. The top inch may stay moist for a week in fairly cool weather, but in hot, windy weather you'll water often, even every day for a plant that needs repotting. That's why well-drained soil is so important. You can pour on the water without drowning the roots.

Mulch will help keep the soil moist and cool. Use a coarse organic mulch such as bark chips and pile it about 2 inches thick. In really hot weather, group your containers. They'll protect each other.

Don't count on rain to do all your watering, since plants in containers may act as umbrellas and shed most of the rain. Check the soil even when rainfall has been abundant. Of course you'll water less, since the moist air will keep water from evaporating.

It is important in any region to leach the soil occasionally. Leaching is long-soaking that dissolves any minerals or salts and flushes them out the drain hole. Well water,

or any water that won't produce good soapsuds or leaves bathtub rings, is heavy with dissolved mineral salts and these deposit in container soil as water evaporates. Eventually you'll see brown leaf edges, then dead leaves, and finally a dead plant. To avoid disaster, put your garden hose in each container every couple of months and let it run slowly for about 20 minutes. It should run just fast enough that the water you add goes through the soil and out the drainhole. Letting it overflow won't add to the effect.

Also, for every watering in hard-water areas, fill the pot until water runs freely from the bottom, go on to other pots, then return and fill the pot a second time. This technique keeps salts to a minimum.

Vacation watering

When you leave home, group your containers near a water source and out of the afternoon sun. The grouping will help keep them moist, the shade will cut the need for water, and if they're near a hose, your vacation waterer won't miss any of them by accident. For large numbers of containers, you can buy water timers that will turn water on at regular intervals. Just hook up a system of small hoses that you place permanently in each container. Drip systems

Half barrels provide ideal homes for 'Southern Sweet' genetic dwarf peaches, leaving room for annual color below.

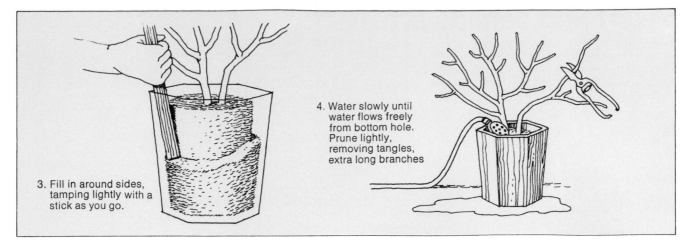

3. Fill in around sides, tamping lightly with a stick as you go.

4. Water slowly until water flows freely from bottom hole. Prune lightly, removing tangles, extra long branches

are effective here too, provided you filter the water before it goes into the system.

Potting and repotting

There are many successful potting methods, and gardeners have great success with methods you'll never see recommended in books. What we suggest here should work every time and keep your plants healthy.

You're aiming for a container soil that holds water but never gets soggy. Water should soak in immediately, never sitting on top, and it should run out just as fast. Choose a synthetic soil or a mixture of synthetic soil and garden loam. Moisten the soil until it's barely damp but not wet. You may find it best to sprinkle and stir the soil one day then pot your plants the next.

Be sure your pot or box has good drain holes. If you buy a container with one small hole, drill two or three more, or ask the nurseryman to do it for you. If you use a can for a season, punch a dozen holes around the bottom with a triangular punch can opener. Cover the holes with broken pieces of pot or broken glass segments, or bits of that old cracked cup you meant to throw out. DON'T fill the bottom with rocks or coarse gravel—they interfere with water flow. The mix should fill the pot from top to bottom.

Place enough soil mix in the pot, lightly tamped down, so the roots touch it when the crown of the plant is just below the pot rim. Hold your bareroot plant at that level and toss in enough soil to support it, tamping lightly as you go, then finish filling to about a quarter inch below the pot rim. The soil will settle, leaving you room to water. An ever-green plant, or any plant in a nursery container, can simply be placed on the first layer of soil. You then fill around it, but before covering the rootball, scratch it all around with a fork to rough up roots and get them pointing outward. Cut off any long, spiraling roots at the bottom.

The repotting technique is similar, and is described in the illustrations here. You repot because any plant tends to bunch feeder roots at the wall of the container. They dry out faster there and the plant lacks water and nutrients even when you care for it properly. When you shave off an inch of root and add fresh soil, the plant can grow healthy young roots and the empty soil around them holds a reservoir of moisture. You must always clip back the top a little when you shave the roots, so that the plant is balanced. New top growth will follow the new root growth.

After potting or repotting, soak the soil thoroughly.

'Washington' navel orange can spend winter indoors.

'Meyer' lemon has flowers, fruit year-round.

Dwarf and semidwarf

Dwarf trees are easy to prune, spray, thin, and harvest, and will often produce a crop years sooner than standard trees. Without the dwarf sizes, many landscape uses of fruiting plants would be difficult, with container plantings of tree fruit almost impossible.

Both the home gardener and commercial orchardist are finding more and more uses for dwarfed fruit trees. On the preceding pages we discuss these uses. Here, we would like to make clear just what the term 'dwarf' means.

Grafted dwarf and genetic dwarf

There are two distinct kinds of dwarf fruit trees; the grafted dwarf that is actually manufactured by the gardener or nurseryman; and the genetic dwarf that is small because of its genetic structure. Meaning, so to speak, it is born that way.

Grafting for small size

When a gardener sets out to create a grafted dwarf, he must first find a plant that will serve as a growth-limiting rootstock. The most extensive research on plants like this has been undertaken with apples, and the illustrations on page 13 will help you see what has been done so far.

The dwarfing part of a grafted dwarf usually consists of the root. The numbered Malling roots, if allowed to grow their own tops, would become slow-growing, shallow-rooted apple trees. When a well-known fruiting apple is grafted to one of these roots, the recalcitrant root doesn't nourish the top as well as ordinary roots might. And since the roots are relatively shallow and don't spread too widely, the mature size of the top is limited.

A propagator can accompish somewhat the same result by grafting the numbered Malling plant to an ordinary root, then grafting a desirable variety to this trunk section. This is called an interstock graft and can be compared to a bottleneck. The ordinary root is vigorous, but the "slow-poke" interstock will only pass along a certain amount of nutrition and the top becomes dwarfed. Interstocks sometimes get very complex, with several kinds of tree making up a single trunk, but most of these three- or four-way grafts are experimental at the present time.

Grafted trees are precocious

The "stingy," dwarfing root or trunk has an important secondary effect on the top beyond dwarfing. A plant that doesn't receive enough nutrients not only grows slowly — it fruits young. Grafted dwarfs usually will have a little fruit on them in their second year.

Choosing a rootstock

Since most of the experimental work on grafted dwarfs has been done with apples, it's no surprise that you have a wide choice of size among apple dwarfs. The M27 rootstock is the most dwarfing, producing apple bushes 4 feet high, but it is not yet widely available.

The M9 root is the most dwarfing among available roots, excellent for containers and informal hedge training. Unfortunately, retail nurseries rarely label the root of a tree separately. You will see the variety name, such as

"If you have space for a rose bush, you have space for a dwarf apple tree," says Fay Paquette, retired horticulturist. "It's like propagating from cuttings, and something anyone can do. I start with two- or three-eye scions and graft them to very thin sections of dwarf root stock, six-inches to eight-inches long. Trees grown in this manner, and pruned back each year, develop short stocky branches and multiple-fruiting spurs. The tree in the photo was a graft of 'Red Delicious' on M.9 rootstock. It is three years old and produced 30 apples after thinning." If you would like to learn more about his grafting methods, you can write to:

Mr. Fay Paquette
2368 Barbara Drive
Camarillo, CA 93010

'Delicious' or 'Melrose' and then 'dwarf' or 'semi-dwarf.' Dwarf means relatively small, while semi-dwarf means relatively large. You can't be sure just what the mature plant will be like.

For containers or formal training it doesn't matter much. You add to the dwarfing effect by your treatment of the plant. For free-standing trees and informal training it can matter a lot, since a 'dwarf' might be a 9-foot M9 or a 15-foot M26. You can solve the problem by buying from a catalog dealer who lists his rootstocks separately, then propagating more rootstocks as needed. A method for doing this is described and illustrated on page 15.

A precaution

However you buy your dwarf trees, it is important never to bury the graft. You will see it on the lower trunk as a bulge with a round scar on one side, or possibly a change of bark texture. If you bury the graft, the top variety will root and grow to full size. The scar should be two inches above the soil. Some nurserymen help you to plant properly by grafting high, about 6 inches above the branching roots or crown. You can bury the lower 3 or 4 inches and still have the graft exposed.

The only exception to the rule of never burying a graft applies to harsh winter areas. Mulch both root and bud union deeply when all growth has stopped in fall, then pull back the mulch when spring growth begins.

Vigorous grafts and slow ones

Beginning on page 98, we discuss grafting techniques, so that you can create your own dwarf orchard from scratch. You can begin in two ways: Either buy grafted dwarfs and add varieties so each tree produces several kinds of fruit; or propagate rootstocks to graft single-variety dwarfs.

Either way, you must consider the vigor of the top varieties. If you mix vigorous and slow branches on the

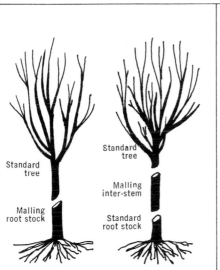

What's a dwarf tree?

A dwarf tree actually consists of 2 or 3 trees. In one type of dwarf, the Malling tree provides the roots, and the standard apple tree provides the fruit. In another type of dwarf, a full sized tree provides the roots, a portion of a Malling tree provides a section of the trunk (interstem), and the standard tree provides the fruit.

Apple tree size differences

To determine the correct spacing of dwarf trees, you should know the natural size of the variety as well as the dwarfing effect of the rootstock. The two charts will help you make this determination.

For instance, the Red Prince Delicious tree is naturally larger than Jonnee. If grown on the same rootstock, Jonnee can be planted closer together than Red Prince. Red Prince on MM 106 should be planted 14 feet apart, while Jonnee on MM 106 is planted at 12-foot intervals.

Or, if you are planting them together, Jonnee should be ordered on a larger rootstock to make best use of the spacing needed for the Red Prince. In this case, Jonnee on MM 111 would fit in the same space as the Red Prince.

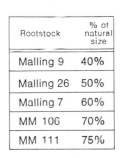

Rootstock	% of natural size
Malling 9	40%
Malling 26	50%
Malling 7	60%
MM 106	70%
MM 111	75%

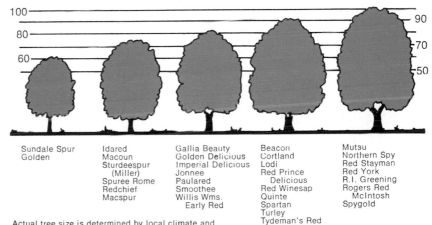

| Sundale Spur Golden | Idared Macoun Sturdeespur (Miller) Spuree Rome Redchief Macspur | Gallia Beauty Golden Delicious Imperial Delicious Jonnee Paulared Smoothee Willis Wms. Early Red | Beacon Cortland Lodi Red Prince Delicious Red Winesap Quinte Spartan Turley Tydeman's Red | Mutsu Northern Spy Red Stayman Red York R.I. Greening Rogers Red McIntosh Spygold |

Actual tree size is determined by local climate and growing conditions. The sizes of these varieties are shown not by feet, but on a relative scale of 100.

The Malling and Merton Malling rootstock numbers determine tree size

M 27 Very dwarfing. Mature trees reach about 4 feet. Hard to find; limited availability.

M 9—Most dwarfing root currently available. (About 9 feet.) Trunk section and root are brittle, so stake free-standing plants. Try to buy trees with bud 6 inches or more above the crown (where roots branch), and plant with bud 2 inches above soil for extra anchoring.

M 26—Less dwarfing than M9 (about 12 feet) unless used in formal espaliers, containers. Fewer suckers than M7.

M 7—Widely available semi-dwarfing root (about 15 feet). Trees budded high and planted deep will sucker less if you can find them. Suckers may be dug or layered for home grafting. Control size by training, pruning.

M M 106—Largest semi-dwarfing rootstock (about 18 feet). Trees can reach ¾ of full size. This root anchors well, suckers very little and resists wooly apple aphid. It is mainly a commercial root stock.

A hedgerow of apples on M9 roots are bent to 45° angle, summer-pruned to increase dwarfing effect of root (see pages 80 and 82).

same tree, the vigorous ones will try to take over. If you mix vigorous and slow varieties in a row of trained dwarfs, the vigorous will be much bigger, since the rootstock won't dwarf them as much.

The chart on page 13 compares a number of vareties on the same rootstock to give you an idea how growth habit changes the ultimate size. The spur varieties will grow the least, while a vigorous 'Cortland' or 'Mutsu' apple will grow perhaps 50 percent larger. The same will happen on a single tree with several grafts unless you match the vigor of the branches.

Wherever possible, we have mentioned the vigor of the varieties named in our variety lists. Before grafting, check to see whether the list gives equal ratings of vigor to the varieties you wish to use.

Other grafted dwarfs

Other major kinds of fruit can be dwarfed by grafting, but far less research has been done, so there are fewer kinds of rootstocks, and they are not always strongly dwarfing.

Pears are dwarfed on quince roots, and since some pears, ('Bartlett' for one) will not join well to quince, an interstock of 'Old Home' pear grows between root and top. Where fireblight is severe, you can sometimes grow a susceptible but tasty variety of pear by letting the 'Old Home' interstock form the whole trunk and the main branches (or scaffold). If a branch catches the blight, it will only die back to the 'Old Home' portion, since 'Old Home' is highly resistant. Finding the 'Old Home' scions to do this may be hard, but try a large wholesale nursery. They may be able to give you scions from their own grafting stock.

Peaches are dwarfed on several rootstocks, especially the Nanking cherry (Prunus tomentosa) and the St. Julien plum. Either root may shorten the life of a tree somewhat.

Plums are sometimes dwarfed on Nanking cherry root, while apricots go onto Western sand cherry (Prunus besseyi). The plants that would normally grow from these roots are shrubby and small, thus their dwarfing effect with the various tops.

Any of these roots can be propagated by the method we describe on page 15, but you can also get more of the same by allowing root suckers to grow, then digging and replanting them during the dormant season. Apple roots don't often send up suckers from underground, but the various stone fruit rootstocks sucker frequently.

Genetic dwarfs are different

The plants called genetic dwarfs are small by nature. There are, however, many forms of them, somtimes more than one form for a single kind of fruit tree.

Among apples, the most common genetic dwarf grows into a fairly large tree. The so called 'spur' apple grows more slowly than the same variety of ordinary apple, produces fewer real branches, but produces many more fruiting spurs. The heavy crops slow its growth a bit more. Even so, a spur apple grows big unless you further dwarf it by grafting.

There is also a very small genetic dwarf apple that is not a spur tree. It is sold as 'Garden Delicious' and has fruit resembling 'Golden Delicious' or 'Mutsu.' In a container you might keep it to three feet, but in the ground it will slowly grow to six or eight feet.

Genetic dwarf peach on its 20th birthday.

Among peaches there is a wide range of genetic dwarfs all related to the Chinese dwarf peaches called 'Swatow' and 'Flory.' These plants grow almost no stem between leaf nodes, so the branches have a typical lumpy look. In the ground you can expect to see these dwarfs reach eight or nine feet, but it will take a while. They are all very decorative, with large, showy flowers; but are fairly tender. Nectarines also grow as short-stemmed dwarfs.

One variety of dwarf peach is a little different. It is a short-stemmed sport discovered in Washington on a 'Redhaven' tree and christened 'Compact Redhaven.' It is not quite as dwarf as the Swatow-Flory series, reaching about 10 feet, but it is quite hardy.

There is also a dwarf apricot and a dwarf sweet cherry. There are several good genetic dwarf sour cherries, including 'Meteor,' 'Northstar,' and 'Mesabi'—all of which are extremely hardy. 'Mesabi' has a sweet cherry among its ancestors, but its fruit is sour. All three grow to perhaps 10 feet under ideal conditions, but more often stay at 6 or 7 feet.

Among plums there are large numbers of natural dwarfs, but these are not plants that bear the familiar varieties. Rather, they are crosses with Western sand cherry or with true cherry and shrub plum. Most of them were developed for very cold climates and are easy to buy in the northern half of the country.

Genetic dwarfs are grafted

You may be surprised to see that your natural dwarf peach is grafted to a large and obviously different rootstock. The root here is not a means of dwarfing. Often it is very vigorous and sends out four-foot suckers almost overnight. Grafting to a rootstock is the only means of producing large numbers of plants for sale. Seed will be of mixed parentage and give a new kind of fruit, so grafting is the way to reproduce any fruit variety, dwarf or standard. However, the vigorous roots (of many kinds) used for dwarf peaches get impatient and grow on their own, so watch for a strange leaf above the normal foliage and tear suckers out at the base. Some nurseries use red-leafed rootstocks to make spotting these intruders easier.

What's better, grafted or genetic?

It's hard to determine whether grafted or genetic dwarfing is best. Neither is actually better, but there are definite advantages to grafting, which is why most of the work of plant scientists concerns rootstocks instead of natural dwarfing.

When you dwarf by grafting, the top can be any variety you like, a good old one, or a problem-solving new one. Scientists work constantly to breed hardy, disease-resistant, or larger, or better fruit, but the developments are slow and frequently disappointing. It simply complicates a difficult job to try to include a dwarf trait along with whatever else you want to see in the offspring. It's easier to work toward one thing at a time and then graft for small size.

The home gardener is also better off with grafted dwarfs in many cases, since his choice of varieties is not limited to fruit he doesn't know. Genetic dwarfs are distinct varieties, different from each other and from standard varieties.

Genetic dwarfs do have advantages. They require no pruning and their fruit tastes perfectly good, if not always top-notch. The peaches and nectarines have another plus: they descend from double-flowered ancestors, providing an extraordinary spring display of flowers. A border or hedge of peach dwarfs is quite a colorful sight during the flowering season.

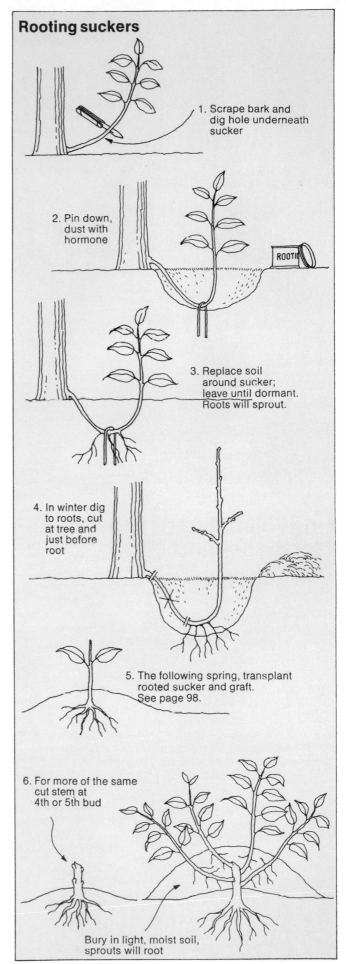

Rooting suckers

1. Scrape bark and dig hole underneath sucker

2. Pin down, dust with hormone

ROOTI

3. Replace soil around sucker; leave until dormant. Roots will sprout.

4. In winter dig to roots, cut at tree and just before root

5. The following spring, transplant rooted sucker and graft. See page 98.

6. For more of the same cut stem at 4th or 5th bud

Bury in light, moist soil, sprouts will root

Longer days and rising temperatures in early spring bring a release of buds from protective dormancy (apple blossoms).

Fruit climates of the Northeast and Midwest

The climates of the northern region of the United States range from the harsh winters and short, cool summers of upper Michigan to the fairly mild coastal climates of New Jersey. At least some varieties of fruit will grow in any of these climate zones, and experienced gardeners probably have a good idea about what they can plant.

Even experienced gardeners, though, may not be up on the latest work of the plant breeders at Experiment Stations and universities in places like New York, Ontario, Minnesota, and South Dakota. To cite just a few examples of their work:

The Durham, New Hampshire, Experiment Station introduced the 'Reliance' peach in 1959, especially for climates where peaches had rarely succeeded before.

The University of Minnesota Fruit Breeding Farm introduced the dwarf cherries 'Meteor' and 'Northstar' in 1950 and 1952, for gardeners in the Plains States, but the two varieties turned out to be quite successful in very mild regions too.

In 1936, Dr. N. E. Hansen of the South Dakota Experiment Station introduced the 'Manchu' apricot, a selection from hardy Siberian natives. Dr. Hansen is well-known for his many introductions of cold-climate varieties, including the Hansen bush cherry. The 'Manchu' apricot became one parent in a cross that produced the 'Sungold' hardy apricot at the University of Minnesota in 1961, together with another selection from the same cross, 'Moongold.' And so the work goes on.

In the variety lists that follow, we have tried to include the best of these new plants, whether they were bred for hardiness, for better fruit, or for sturdier growth, but there are new introductions all the time.

Plant researchers have gone in another direction that helps in climate control. The many new dwarf fruit plants, whether natural or grafted, can help you beat the weather, since they grow well in containers and can be moved inside when the weather turns bleak.

Of course you'll want to look into the most up-to-date varieties and planting techniques, but the old methods of weather protection are still important. Here is a list of weather dangers and what to do about them:

✔Extreme cold. Choose the hardiest varieties, then cover the root zone with heavy mulch in winter—six inches or more. Pin the mulch down with wire or boughs so wind won't carry it away. Damage from cold varies by season. A completely dormant plant takes cold better than one that has begun to grow again. Flower buds are particularly sensitive. Plant where cold air can flow away from your fruit garden so that warming spring days aren't followed by nights in a hollow filled with arctic air.

✔Wind. Wind dries your plants at a time of year when water may be trapped in the ground as ice. Drought is a serious hazard during winter. And of course, wind can snap off branches. If you have no naturally protected site for planting, put in an evergreen windbreak when you put in your orchard. A windbreak of trees is more effective than a solid barrier such as a fence, since the wind can't flow over the top in a solid wave and crash down on the other side. For temporary wind protection use snow fencing or burlap tacked to stakes.

The date when spring arrives changes from year to year, but the sequence of bloom is always the same (pear blossoms).

✔ Sun. The first strong sun can do serious damage to plants that are still leafless. Protect them from sunburn by painting the trunk and main branches with white interior latex paint.

✔ Ice. You can't do much about an ice storm, but do tap off snow and icicles before they build up enough to break branches.

The zones of our map

The map on the following pages is divided into five zones by bands of color. Each band suggests the approximate length of the growing season for fruit plants. In general, if you live in a northerly or inland portion of any zone, your climate will be more severe and your season shorter.

Zone 1. The coldest areas of northern New England. The short growing season and late frosts limit the choice of fruit plants to the hardiest varieties. Apples are among the best tree crops. Consider dwarf trees in containers that can live indoors for part of the year.

Zone 2. Corresponds to Zone 1, except in the Central States where wind may be more intense and snow cover less trustworthy. This is the zone where the new hardy fruit plants show their worth.

Zone 3. From the southern Great Lakes in Michigan, Ohio, and New York, and in some coastal areas of New England the presence of water tempers the climate, making winter less harsh and summer longer. The fruit belt of the southern portion of Michigan is typical. Commercial orchards there produce cherries, peaches, and many other fruits. You can choose any temperate-zone fruit here and hope for success, although even here you'll need the hardiest apricots, and fairly hardy plums and peaches.

Zone 4. Fruit crops do well in this area if you protect them from the worst of the weather. The growing season is long, but occasional extremes can cause damage.

Zone 5. Particularly favored. In the mildest coastal portions, gardeners can even try a fig tree in a warm corner.

Chart symbols

The following is an explanation of the symbols used on the next page.

★ (star). This means that the varieties listed may be planted.

H—Hardy varieties. Choose the most cold-tolerant fruits in our lists. Some representative plants in this group: Apple—'Red Baron'; Pear—'Clapp's Favorite'; Peach 'Reliance'; Plum—'Superior'; Apricot—'Goldcot'; Cherry—'Meteor.'

U—Uncertain crops. Even where hardy fruiting plants survive, extreme cold or late frost will sometimes destroy the blossoms or young fruit. Plants with a "U" listing will do somewhat better if you choose a climate-moderating planting site, like a south facing wall.

wp—Needs special winter protection. Dwarf apples and pears should have deep winter mulch. Where snow cover is uncertain, hold the mulch in place with fence wire or evergreen boughs. Spread the mulch four to six inches deep from branch tip to trunk. Some plants such as strawberry, raspberry, and grape can be buried in mulch after the first cold stops all growth.

no symbol—plant not advised. Plants may lack a symbol for two reasons: Either they are too tender for the district (blackberry in the coldest areas), or they can be replaced by superior but more tender varieties (cherry plum in Southern Michigan).

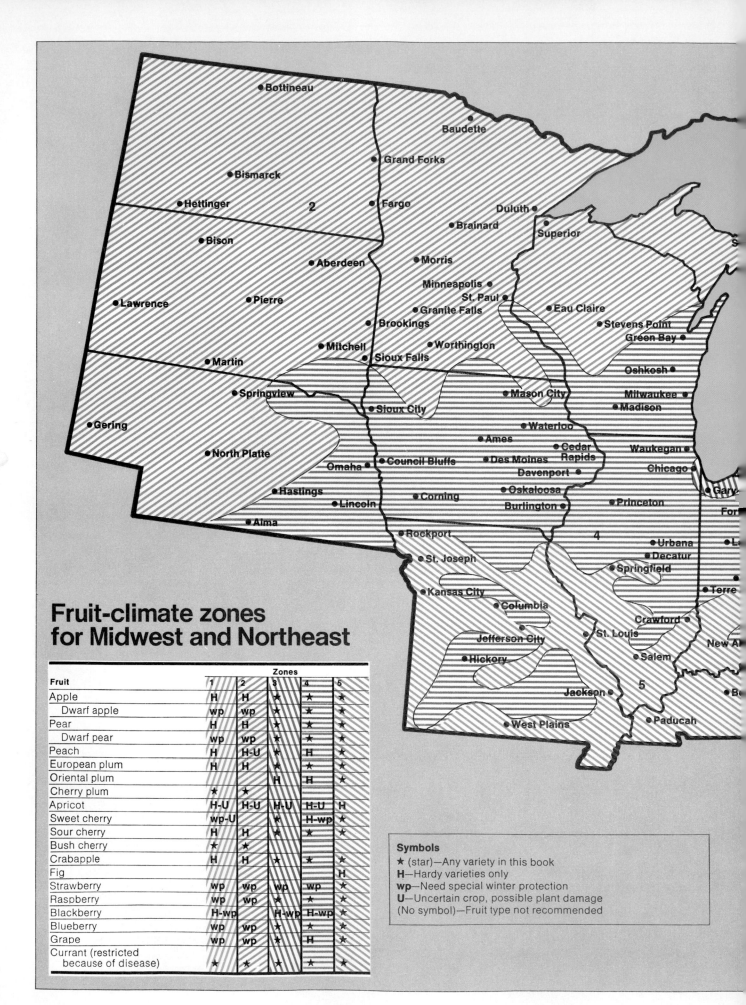

Fruit-climate zones for Midwest and Northeast

Fruit	Zones				
	1	2	3	4	5
Apple	H	H	★	★	★
Dwarf apple	wp	wp	★	★	★
Pear	H	H	★	★	★
Dwarf pear	wp	wp	★	★	★
Peach	H	H-U	★	H	★
European plum	H	H	★	★	★
Oriental plum			H	H	★
Cherry plum	★	★			
Apricot	H-U	H-U	H-U	H-U	H
Sweet cherry	wp-U		★	H-wp	★
Sour cherry	H	H	★		★
Bush cherry	★	★			
Crabapple	H	H	★	★	★
Fig					H
Strawberry	wp	wp	wp	wp	★
Raspberry	wp	wp	★	★	★
Blackberry	H-wp		H-wp	H-wp	★
Blueberry	wp	wp	★	★	★
Grape	wp	wp	★	H	★
Currant (restricted because of disease)	★	★	★	★	★

Symbols

★ (star)—Any variety in this book
H—Hardy varieties only
wp—Need special winter protection
U—Uncertain crop, possible plant damage
(No symbol)—Fruit type not recommended

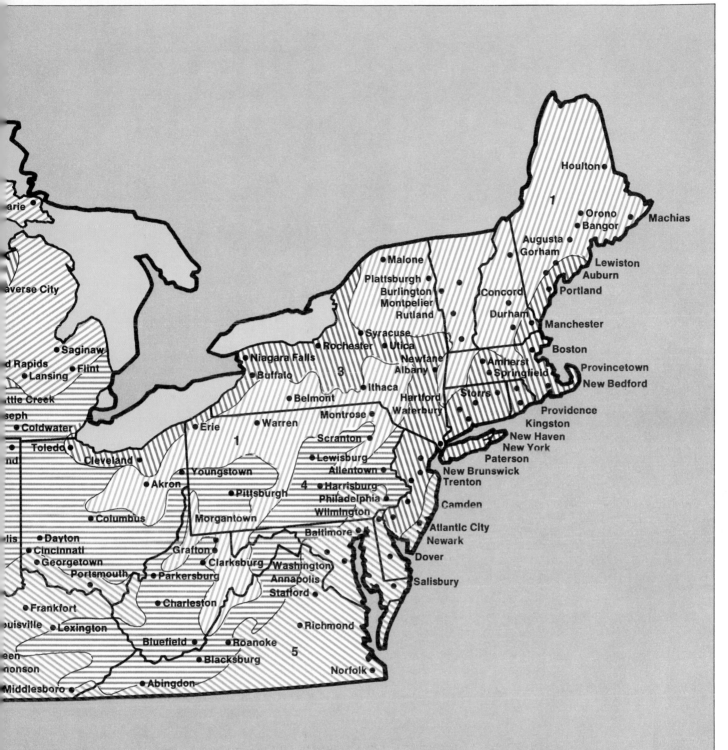

Key to Chart

ZONE 1—Growing season from 90 to 150 days, moderate summer temperatures.

ZONE 2—Growing season from 90 to 150 days. Similar to Zone 1 but more severe.

ZONE 3—Growing season 150 to 180 days. Climate tempered by bodies of water.

ZONE 4—Growing season 150 to 180 days. Similar to Zone 3, but inland, severe.

ZONE 5—Growing season 180 to 210 days. Tempered by river valleys, coast.

Tree fruits

**For the suburban garden or the high-rise patio terrace,
there's a fruit tree to fit your needs.
You can forget the orchard these days and choose fruit for
the living-space garden.**

The information in this chapter will help you choose the fruit tree that's right for you in every respect.

Using the introductions

Each variety list is preceded by an introduction. Use these paragraphs as a kind of expanded index to the rest of the book. We give you page references to the more detailed sections on landscaping, pruning, and grafting.

In the early paragraphs we tell you what sizes of plants are available, from standard through the various dwarfs, grafted or genetic. Following this, we discuss space-saving methods of planting and training.

Each kind of fruit bears its crop in a slightly different way, and you have to understand the where and how when you prune or train a plant. The discussion here includes sketches to help you find the fruiting wood on your own plants.

We also tell you how much pruning you can expect to do, and whether you should thin out the young fruit for a better crop.

The variety lists

The material under each variety name will give you a lot of information. Here's what you'll find.

1. The time of harvest: Fruits like apples, with varieties that bear over a very long season, are grouped under headings such as 'Early' or 'Midseason.' If all varieties fruit at nearly the same time, you'll find the information within the entry.

2. Place of origin of the variety: Many varieties are the result of modern plant-breeding experiments that suit them to a special climate. An apple or cherry developed by Minnesota breeders will take hard winters. We tell you if it does well in other climates too.

3. A description of the fruit: The entry mentions what it looks like, outside and inside, and many entries suggest the best uses, whether fresh, for cooking, or for canning.

4. A description of the tree: You'll find out whether the tree is especially vigorous or weak, productive, good-looking, or disease-resistant.

5. Best region for the variety: Some varieties are meant for special climates. The 'Red Baron' apple, 'Reliance' peach, and 'Moongold' apricot are for extreme winters and we say so. If the fruit is widely adapted you won't see a special mention.

6. Special information: Some peaches have big pink flowers that show off well in the landscape. We mention that, and we'll also mention anything special about pollination when one variety differs from the rest.

7. Availability: The numbers following each variety refer to our catalog list on page 111. You can order direct from many of these dealers, or ask your nurseryman to order from wholesalers. After some numbers you'll see a small 's' or capital 'D.' That means the dealer sells semidwarf or dwarf plants. If a variety is sold almost everywhere, we say merely that it is widely distributed

Espaliers take little space, but provide lots of flowers and fruit.

Small size is no indication of harvest, as the owner enjoys a bountiful crop of apples.

Apples

For some people the only apple is a polished red one. Others must have a striped apple, or a golden, or a tart green apple for pies. Many remember a particular tree with some antique variety on its mossy branches. We've tried to satisfy these cravings and memories by presenting our varieties in a double list. First you'll find the more common fruits such as 'Delicious,' 'McIntosh,' and 'Jonathan' and the sports of these that vary mainly in color and bearing habit. Many apple varieties are really members of a group, with 'Delicious' alone counting many sports with redder fruit, more spurs on the branches, and larger fruit size.

In the same list you'll find the newest hybrids, just right for some special tricky climate, and recent imports such as 'Mutsu' from Japan.

A second list follows, under the heading Old Apples. These are fruits that have been around for hundreds of years, but are now less common in the nursery and commercial trade. One of them may be the fruit you remember from childhood.

The size of the tree

Plant scientists in England and elsewhere have done extensive work on dwarfing rootstocks for apples, so plant size ranges from a 4-foot bush to a 30-foot spreading tree. There is even a true, or genetic, dwarf these days that stays small on any rootstock. Since the subject is complex, you'll find a detailed discussion and silhouettes of comparative sizes on page 13 under the Merton and Malling heading.

Dwarfing rootstocks make it easy for a gardener to control size even further by special pruning and training. Apples can now grow in boxes, flat on a wall or trellis, as hedges, or in fanciful three-dimensional shapes. Look for training methods under the heading Space-Saver Training on page 79 and following.

Let us repeat here what we have said elsewhere about rootstocks. You may not be able to find labelled roots in your retail nursery. The nurseryman will say 'dwarf' or 'semidwarf.' The natural size of these trees covers the whole range of our silhouettes, but even the larger sizes

'Red Delicious'

can be successfully dwarfed still further by a container or a space-saver training method. It's good to know what root you have bought, but not absolutely crucial.

Small-space planting

Apples bear on long-lived spurs, so heavy pruning won't remove your crop. That means that any training method we mention in these pages will suit an apple variety. Put the young trees in the ground at a 45-degree angle and keep them pruned for a fruit-filled hedge, or have an orchard in boxes on your patio. Adapt the formal training described following page 78 and you can grow apples into the shape of a pergola or summerhouse and give tea parties behind apple walls.

Apples are also among the easiest fruit plants to graft, and a beginner can feel like an expert when he succeeds in producing a 10-variety tree on the first try. All methods are

Through the seasons this Gravenstein espalier needs care. For scale and scab, spray in winter and at bud break.

'Jonnee,' a sport of 'Jonathan'

'Golden Delicious'

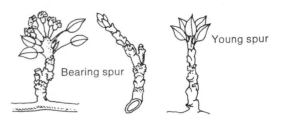

Bearing spur

Young spur

suitable, but for a tree that is fairly young, the T-bud and whip methods are the easiest. If you practice a little first, you can place buds along the trunk of a young whip and train them formally for a multiple-variety espalier. See the Space-Saver section for details, but instead of encouraging natural buds, add grafted ones.

Where does the fruit grow?

The sketch above will show you how an apple spur looks and bears. The fruit forms at the tip of last year's spur growth, and the spur itself then grows a bit more, off to the side of the fruit. Each spur bears for 10 years or more, so don't tear it off when you pick. For comparison, the straight spur at the right has not yet borne fruit.

You will hear about spur varieties. These are sports of a number of standard varieties, often of 'Delicious' or 'McIntosh' but there are others. They grow less each season, and their spurs are packed closer together on the branch. The less vigorous growth means that they are a kind of genetic dwarf, but they are still good-sized trees unless grafted to dwarfing roots. One caution: spur varieties are difficult to handle for the really formal training methods. If you buy spur varieties on dwarfing roots, use an informal training method that doesn't call for any particular form.

Pruning an apple

Pruning methods depend on how you grow the tree. For special training, turn to page 82. For general pruning of the larger dwarfed trees or standard trees, see the pruning pages.

Apart from special training, here are basic guides: The smallest dwarfs should be trained to branch very low, and if they are not otherwise supported they should be staked. Larger trees should be trained to a strong basic scaffold, and the oldest branches (usually dangling) should be pruned off when age or shade from upper branches cuts their production of fruit. Trim back to a more vertical branch.

Thinning the fruit

Thinning is crucial with many apple varieties. They overset, and the heavy crop can snap branches. Even more important, many apple varieties tend to bear every other year. If you leave too much fruit you encourage alternate bearing, and the following year you may find that your tree bears only a handful of apples.

There are many thinning methods, but the most direct is to wait for the natural drop of young fruit in June, then thin the remaining fruit so that there is a single apple every six inches along the branches. Each spur may have a cluster of fruit. A single fruit is less likely to become diseased so

Wait for petal fall to spray for codling moth. Thin the fruit at thumbnail size to one a spur.

Note the characteristic 'Delicious' shape.

'Tydeman's Red,' a 'McIntosh' type.

Great for cooking, this is 'Golden Delicious.'

'Cortland,' another 'McIntosh' descendant.

leave only the largest fruit on each spur. Thin carefully or you will damage the spurs.

Pollination

Apples are only partially self-fruitful, but many varieties set a good crop without a pollinator. Any two kinds that bloom together offer cross-pollination (with some exceptions listed below). If you plant only a very early and a very late variety, they will not cross-pollinate.

A few apples have infertile pollen. The following will not set a crop at all if you plant them together with no other source of pollen: 'Gravenstein,' 'Stayman' (and 'Stayman' sports such as 'Blaxstayman' and 'Staymared'), and 'Winesap.'

Winter chill

All apples need some cool winter weather, but there is an enormous range in this requirement, so varieties are available for any climate except subtropical and low desert regions.

Pests and disease

Apples are subject to attack by a good many organisms, but the gardener will have most trouble with codling moth and other fruit-spoiling pests, and then with the usual aphids, mites, scale, and so forth. See the pest and disease section for further details. A regular spray schedule is best. A fungicide will control diseases such as mildew and scab where they are a problem.

The variety list

Our list is divided by bearing season and further divided into two sections. First you will find the best of today's varieties, then a list of old apple varieties. Catalog numbers at the end of each entry include a small 's' where semi-dwarf trees are sold, and a 'D' for dwarf trees.

Early season

'Lodi.' Origin: Geneva, NY. A cross of 'Montgomery' and 'Yellow Transparent.' Fruit is medium to large, up to 3 inches in diameter. The skin is light green, sometimes with a slight orange blush. The flesh is nearly white, with a slightly greenish tinge, fine grained, tender and juicy, and sour. The eating quality is only fair, but its kitchen quality is excellent. Use in sauce and for pies. An alternate bearer, 'Lodi' is noted for its tendency to overset fruit and must be thinned early. Widely available.

'Yellow Transparent.' Introduced from Russia almost 100 years ago, it is still valued by a discriminating, loyal following for quality as an early green cooking apple. Fruit is medium in size and shape. The skin is greenish-yellow and the flesh is white tinged greenish-yellow. It does show bruises readily and soon becomes overmature. The flesh texture is fine-grained, crisp, and juicy. Eating quality is good and kitchen quality is excellent for sauce and in pies. An annual bearer. Widely available.

'Summerred.' Origin: Summerland, British Columbia, Can. A cross of 'McIntosh' and 'Golden Delicious.' A medium-to-large apple, oblong-conic in shape. Skin has bright, solid red blush with prominent dots. Flesh is fine in texture, soft, with a sharp, full, flavor. Good eating fresh and in sauce and pies. A strong upright grower, bears annually, requires thinning. Available: (7s), (10), (28), (43sD).

'Niagara.' Origin: Geneva, NY. A cross of 'Carlton' and 'McIntosh.' Fruit is of the 'McIntosh' type in appearance

'Prima,' is scab resistant.

Half 'Jonathan,' half 'Golden Delicious' equals 'Jonagold.'

'Melrose' resembles 'Jonathan' parent.

'Jonamac' shows 'McIntosh' influence.

and flavor. Ripens two weeks before 'McIntosh,' Tree growth habit and productivity similar to 'McIntosh'—Strong, very vigorous. Available: (28).

'Oriole.' Origin: Minnesota. Large, roundish fruit. Skin is orange-yellow in color, striped with red. Flesh is fine-grained and tender, juicy, and aromatic. Excellent for eating fresh and for sauce, or quartered for pies. Tree is medium-tall, vigorous, and rounded in shape. Available: (12), (43sD).

'Early McIntosh.' Origin: Geneva, NY. A cross of 'Yellow Transparent' and 'McIntosh.' Skin is a very good red. Excellent eaten fresh, for sauce, and for pies. However, the tree is very difficult for the average grower to thin and size. Available: (2s), (25sD), (27s), (34), (35sD), (48sD).

'Duchess.' An early bearer of red-striped, medium-sized fruit. Flavor is tart. Good for sauce and quartered for pies. Available: (29), (32sD).

'Melba.' Origin: Canada. Very hardy, annual bearing, medium-to-large fruit. Skin is light green with red blush. Flesh is white, fine-textured, tender and crisp. Available: (23D), (25sD).

'Puritan.' Origin: Massachusetts. A cross of 'McIntosh' and 'Red Astrachan.' Fruit is medium-sized and uniformly round in shape. Skin is an attractive solid red. Flesh is white, tender, fairly soft, a bit tart but of very good quality. Tree is medium-sized, moderately vigorous, with wide crotch angles and well branched. Bears alternately. Available: (1s), (23), (44sD).

'Wellington.' Origin: Geneva, NY. A cross of 'Crimson Beauty' and 'Cortland.' Fruit is large, with red-striped,

attractive skin. Essentially a sauce apple. Tree is upright, and spreading. Bears annually. Available: (32sD).

'Gravenstein.' Large, but not uniform fruit. Skin is red-striped with light green ground. Flesh is greenish-yellow, moderately fine-textured, crisp, firm, and juicy. Tree is strong and very vigorous, with an upright, spreading growth habit. An excellent variety for eating out-of-hand, for sauce, and quartered for pies. Bears alternately. Widely available.

Early to midseason

'Tydeman's Red.' Origin: England. A 'McIntosh' type, ripening four weeks earlier than the 'McIntosh.' Fruits are almost entirely red from a very early stage. Shaped like a 'McIntosh,' they should be picked within a period of a few days for optimum dessert quality and distinctive flavor, and because they drop quickly at maturity. Fruits are of a good eating quality and keep in storage much longer than most early varieties. The fruit's virtue is early ripening when few other varieties are being harvested. A drawback is growth habit—the branches are long and lanky and need to be controlled by pruning. Grow on dwarf or semidwarf rootstocks. An annual bearer. Widely available.

'Paulared.' Origin: Michigan. This variety is rated high on several counts. It has eye appeal—a solid red blush with a bright yellow ground color. Excellent, slightly tart flavor, good for eating fresh and in sauce and pies. White-to-cream flesh is nonbrowning. The tree is everything an attractive tree should be—strong upright, with good branch structure. Ripens early, about two weeks before 'McIntosh.' Although it colors early, it should not be picked until nearly mature if you want a quality apple. An annual bearer, fruit holds well on the tree and is harvested in two pickings. Has long storage life. Available: (22sD), (44sD).

'Prima.' This new variety is scab-resistant—a virtue that dramatically reduces the need for sprays. Fruit is medium-to-large, and round in shape. The skin is a medium dark red over bright yellow. Flesh is yellowish, firm, crisp, fine-grained, and juicy. Both a good eating and cooking apple. Bears a good crop every year. Fruits may hang on the tree and become overripe. Available: (25s), (34D), (44sD).

'Jonathan.' The standard 'Jonathan' is one of the top varieties produced by commercial growers in the Central States. The fruit is medium-sized, uniform. Skin is washed red and pale yellow, with firm, crisp, juicy flesh, with a rich flavor that makes it a good choice for snacks, salads, and all culinary uses. Widely available.

There are several new 'Jonathan' types to consider. Among them are:

'Jonagold.' Origin: Geneva, NY. A cross of 'Jonathan' and 'Golden Delicious,' a beautiful large apple with a lively, yellow-green ground color partly covered with bright red stripes. Cream-colored flesh is crisp and juicy with good flavor. It is a dual-purpose apple—good for cooking, and eating quality is among the very best. Stores well. The trees are vigorous and annually productive; sturdy, with wide-angled branches. Available: (27s), (28), (32sD), (43sD), (48sD).

'Jonamac.' A 'McIntosh' type dessert apple. The eating quality is very good. Milder in flavor than the 'McIntosh.' Bears annually. Available: (28), (48sD).

Midseason varieties

'Wealthy.' A hardy old variety. Good for eating and cooking. A long bloom period in midseason makes it a good pollinator for most varieties. Fruit is medium to large, uniform, rough. Flesh is white stained with pink, fine-textured, firm, tender, tart, and juicy. Eating quality is good and kitchen quality is excellent for sauce and good for pies, baking, and stewing. An alternate bearer. Available: (12D), (17D), (20D), (25sD), (26), (27s), (29), (44sD).

'Wayne.' Origin: Geneva, NY. A cross of 'Northwestern Greening' and 'Red Spy.' Fruit is large, solidly blushed and washed light scarlet. Excellent for sauce, or eaten fresh, and for desserts and salads. Tree is upright and spreading. Available: (2), (28), (32sD).

'Minjon.' Origin: Minnesota. A cross of 'Wealthy' and 'Jonathan.' Fruit is below medium in size. Skin is dark, solid red in color and the flesh is often pink or stained red. Tart in flavor, it is good eaten fresh, used for sauce, pies, and baking. Tree is very hardy and vigorous; requires thinning. Available: (12), (29).

'Haralson.' Origin: Minnesota. Fruit is medium-sized and round in shape. Skin is an attractive red with greenish dots. Flesh is white, firm, moderately tender, juicy, and tart. Good for eating fresh; also for sauce, pies, and baking. Stores well. Tree is hardy, vigorous, and upright-growing. Available: (12D), (13), (17D), (20D), (26), (29).

'Macoun.' Origin: Geneva, NY. This annual-bearing variety received a new burst of interest in the early 1970's because of its very excellent fresh eating quality. A cross of 'McIntosh' and 'Jersey Black,' the fruit is similar to 'McIntosh' but smaller. Skin is very dark red in color. Flesh is white, richly flavored, aromatic; high dessert quality. Tree is upright-growing, with long, lanky branches. Thinning aids in attaining good fruit size and annual cropping. Widely available.

'Cortland' is white under the red skin.

'Empire.' Origin: Geneva, NY. Cross between 'McIntosh' and 'Delicious.' Fruit is medium and uniform. Skin is dark red, striped, with whitish-cream flesh that is firm, medium-textured, crisp, and very juicy. Eating quality is excellent. One of its major faults is that it develops full color long before it has become harvest-mature, tempting the grower to harvest too early. Trees are moderately vigorous, upright-spreading in form, and annual-bearing. Available: (1s), (2s), (27s), (28), (32D), (44sD), (48sD).

Midseason to late

'Newtown Pippin.' A midseason (bordering on late) variety. Fruit is medium in size with greenish yellow skin and crisp, firm flesh. Tree has a strong, very vigorous growth habit. Kitchen quality is good fresh; excellent for sauce and quartered for pies. Widely available.

'Delicious.' A late-bearing variety. Medium-sized fruit that is long and tapering in shape. Skin is striped-to-solid red with slightly yellow, firm flesh that is juicy, sweet, and aromatic. The most important variety grown in the U.S. Hand thinning is usually necessary to produce apples of good size and dessert quality. Widely available.

'Fireside.' A late-bearing variety. Large fruit, up to 3 inches in diameter. Skin is medium red, lightly striped with darker red. Flesh is yellowish, medium-coarse, tender, and juicy. An excellent variety for dessert purposes. Tree is vigorous and hardy. Available: (12sD), (17), (29).

'Idared.' A cross of 'Jonathan' and 'Wagener.' Fruit skin is an attractive, nearly solid red, with a smooth finish. Fruit is large and uniform, with white, firm, smooth-textured flesh. Excellent dessert and cooking quality. Long storage life. Tree is strong, vigorous, upright; very productive. Bears annually, late season. Widely available.

'McIntosh.' If you write down the attributes of a great apple—"medium to large fruits, white flesh, sweet, tender and juicy, very good eaten fresh, in sauce, in pies, or as a cider variety"—you would have the 'McIntosh.' The skin is yellow, with a bright red blush. The tree is an annual bearer, with a strong, very vigorous growth habit. Widely available.

'Cortland.' Origin: Geneva, NY. According to many apple growers, 'Cortland' rates "excellent" as a dual-purpose variety. "It's better than 'McIntosh,' " they say. Bears heavy annual crops of large red-striped fruit with white flesh which, when exposed to air, is slow to turn brown, making it especially suited for use in salads. The tree has a strong, very vigorous, spreading, drooping growth habit. Widely available.

'Priscilla.' One of the two new scab-resistant varieties

'Mutsu' descends from 'Golden Delicious.' From Japan.

and a good partner in the same orchard with 'Prima,' since it serves as a good pollinator. Fruit is large and slightly rounded. Skin has bright red blush over yellow ground. Flesh is white to slightly greenish in color, with a crisp, medium texture. It is good eating fresh, and will store up to three months. The tree has a moderately vigorous growth habit. Available: (2s), (34D), (44sD).

'Rhode Island Greening.' Still rated at or near the top as a cooking or processing variety after more than 200 years. Fruit is light green to yellow, firm-fleshed, crisp, and juicy. A top-quality cooking apple, good for sauces and baking. Generally a good cropper, but poor pollinator. Bears late, and in alternate years. Available: (23), (25sD), (27s), (28s), (32sD), (44sD).

Late varieties

'Golden Delicious.' For a great dual-purpose, eating, and cooking apple, 'Golden Delicious' ranks as high as any. Fruit is medium-to-large and uniform in size. The skin is greenish-yellow with bright pink blush. Flesh is firm, crisp, juicy, and sweet. The eating quality is excellent fresh and in desserts and salads. It makes a very good grade of sauce. The tree is medium in height, moderately vigorous, upright, round-headed, with wide-angle crotches. It bears very young and ripens late in the season. Bears annually, if thinned. Widely available.

'Mutsu.' Origin: Japan. Cross of 'Golden Delicious' and the Japanese variety 'Indo.' This newcomer has gained the approval of both the grower and consumer. Large, oblong, greenish fruits develop some yellow color when mature. The flesh is coarse-textured, firm, and crisp. Excellent flavor (more tart than 'Golden Delicious') when eaten fresh. Rated high for sauce, pies, and as a baked apple. 'Mutsu,' unlike 'Golden Delicious' does not shrivel in storage. The flesh is coarse-textured, firm, and crisp. Excellent crops annually. Available: (2s), (23D), (28), (32sD), (43sD), (44sD), (48sD).

'Rome Beauty.' "The world's best baking apple." Many red sports with a beautiful, solid, medium-dark-red color. Fruit is large and round, with medium-textured, firm, crisp flesh. The tree is moderately vigorous, and a heavy annual producer. It comes into production at an early age. Fruit has a long storage life. Widely available.

'King.' Origin: North Carolina. A high-quality apple for eating fresh or for use in the kitchen. Fruit is very large and deep red. Flesh is pure white, firm, crisp, sweet, and juicy. Excellent for eating out-of-hand, and for use in pies and sauce. The tree is weak, slow-growing, and semidwarf in habit. Annual bearer. Available: (27s), (28), (32sD), (35D).

'Stayman.' Very late ripener. Where it can be grown, the 'Stayman' is good for cooking or eating fresh. The fruit is juicy with a moderately tart, rich, wine-like flavor. It is fine-textured, firm, and crisp. Skin is bright red. However, skin "cracking" is one drawback. Tree is medium-sized and moderately vigorous. Annual bearer. Widely available.

'Northern Spy.' Trees are very slow to come into bearing; sometimes fourteen years elapse before they bear their first bushel. Alternate-bearing. Fruit is large, with skin of yellow and red stripes. Flesh is yellowish, firm, and crisp. Excellent quality fresh and quartered for pies. Fruit bruises easily. Fruit has a long storage life. Trees are vigorous in their growth habit. Widely available.

'Prairie Spy.' Origin: Minnesota. A late-bearing variety. Fruit is large. Skin is striped red, with crisp, juicy flesh. High dessert and culinary quality. Tree is hardy and vigorous. Available: (12), (17), (29).

'Redwell.' Origin: Minnesota. An annual-bearing variety. Fruit is medium-to-large in size; rounded shape. Skin is very attractive, bright medium-red over yellow, but tends to bruise easily. Flesh is cream-colored, mild, and tender; good for baking, dessert, sauce. Tree is medium-sized with strong framework; hardy. Available: (12).

'Red Delicious.' Everyone knows that 'Red Delicious' is the number-one apple in the supermarket. There is no question about the quality of 'Red Delicious' as a dessert and eating out-of-hand apple. Fruit is medium-to-large. Skin color is striped to full red and the flesh is moderately firm in texture. Your best choices are the red sports such as 'Wellspur' or 'Royal Red.' Tree tends to produce full crops every other year unless properly thinned. Widely available.

'Spartan.' Origin: Summerland, British Columbia, Canada. Cross between 'McIntosh' and 'Newton.' Fruit is medium size, uniform, and symmetrical in shape. Skin is a solid dark red. Flesh is light yellow, firm, tender, crisp, and juicy. Strictly a dessert variety. Tree is strong, moderately vigorous, and well shaped. Must be thinned to assure good size and annual bearing. Widely available.

'Melrose.' Origin: Ohio. A cross between 'Jonathan' and 'Delicious.' Resembles the 'Jonathan' in color and shape, but is less tart. Rate it high as a home-orchard apple for eating out-of-hand, for use in sauce and pies, and for exceptional storage qualities. Fruit is large, uniform, and somewhat flat in shape. The skin is yellow with a bright red wash. Flesh is firm, tender, and crisp. Fruit won't polish like a well-known 'Red Delicious.' On all counts, except color, it out-rates the 'Red Delicious.' The tree is medium in height, moderately vigorous, upright, and spreading. Available: (2s), (8D), (28), (32sD), (43sD), (44sD).

'Spigold.' Origin: Geneva, NY. A cross of 'Northern Spy' and 'Golden Delicious.' Fruit is very large, beautifully colored with bright red stripes on a golden yellow background. The flesh is crisp, delicately flavored, and most pleasing to the taste. An excellent variety for eating fresh and for desserts and salads. Tree grows more vigorously than most varieties and produces good crops at an early age, when grown as a semidwarf. Alternate-bearing. Available: (27s), (28), (32sD), (48sD).

'Monroe.' Origin: Geneva, NY. A cross of 'Jonathan' and 'Rome Beauty.' Fruit is medium to large, roundish, with nearly solid red skin. Flesh is yellowish, firm, crisp, and juicy. Used primarily for cooking. Tree is medium-sized, vigorous, upright, and spreading. A reliable annual bearer; very productive. Available: (28).

'Holly.' A heavy bearer of red, crisp fruit. Flesh is juicy and sweet. Available: (28).

'Northwestern Greening.' A producer of very large, green or yellow fruit. Good for sauce, and quartered for pies. Available: (1sS), (12), (17), (29), (44sD).

'Red Duchess.' Producer of medium-size, red fruit. Good for sauce, quartered for pies, and for jam and jelly stock. Available: (29), (32sD).

Extra hardy

In cold winter areas where some of the favorite apple varieties are subject to winter damage, three hardy varieties developed by the University of Minnesota have an important place.

'Red Baron.' Origin: Minnesota. Cross of 'Golden Delicious' and 'Red Duchess.' Fruit is medium-sized and round in shape. The skin is cherry red, and the flesh is crisp and juicy, with a pleasantly tart flavor. Quality is good eaten out-of-hand, or for making sauce and pies. Available: (12).

'Honeygold.' Origin: Minnesota. This variety boasts a 'Golden Delicious' flavor. The fruit is medium-to-large with golden to yellow-green skin and yellow, crisp, smooth, tender, juicy flesh. Good eating fresh and in sauce and pies. The tree has a moderately vigorous growth habit. Available: (12).

'Regent.' Origin: Minnesota. For a long-keeping red winter apple, 'Regent' is recommended. Fruit is medium in size, with bright red skin and creamy white juicy flesh. The texture is crisp. Rated excellent for cooking or eating, it retains its fine dessert quality late into winter. The tree has a vigorous growth habit and is an annual bearer. Available: (12D), (44sD).

Old apples

The list below includes fine old varieties that are now rare in the commercial and nursery trade. We list the availability of plants by number, with numbers referring to our catalogue list, but you can also order scions for grafting. Write to the Worcester County Horticultural Society, 30 Elm Street, Worcester, Mass. 01608, for a descriptive list and order blank.

Early season

'Early Harvest.' Origin: Unknown. Tree is medium-sized, with an upright, spreading, roundish, and open growth habit. Fruit is medium-sized and nearly round in shape. Skin is pale yellow, smooth, and waxen. Flesh is white and has a soft, fine, tender-to-crisp texture. Excellent eaten fresh and for desserts and salads. Fruit is not a good keeper, and bruises easily. Bears alternately and annually, taking 4 to 6 years to the first crop. Available: (32sD).

'Red Astrachan.' Origin: Russia. A medium-sized tree, upright and spreading growth habit. Fruit is medium-sized and roundish in shape. Skin is yellow splashed dark red. Flesh is white, often strongly tinged red. An excellent cooking apple, and when fully ripe very desirable eaten fresh or for desserts and salads, though very perishable. Tree bears young, moderately, and sometimes annually. Available: (2s), (2sD), (10), (27), (28s), (32sD).

'White Astrachan.' Origin: Russia. A vigorous-growing tree, with a full, well-rounded crown, it needs moderate pruning. Bears medium-sized round fruit. Skin is green and yellow with pink stripes or blush. Flesh is white, crisp, and tart. A very good apple for all culinary uses. Bears annually, taking 7 years to the first crop. Available: (10), (15).

Midseason

'Chenango' ('Chenango Strawberry'). Origin: New York. A medium-sized tree, with an upright, roundish, and spreading growth habit. Fruit is medium to large. The yellow and white skin is striped red. Flesh is white, firm, tender, very aromatic, and juicy. Use for cooking and eating raw. Does not keep well in storage, having a tendency to lose color. Annual-bearing over several weeks. Takes 4 to 6 years to first crop. Available: (25sD), (27s), (28s), (32sD).

'Palmer Greening' ('Washington Royal'). Origin: Sterling, Massachusetts. Tree has an upright, spreading-to-roundish growth habit. Fruit is medium- to above-average-sized. Skin is waxy and greenish-yellow, shaded red. Flesh is

English 'Cox Orange' tastes fine fresh or cooked.

'Fameuse' from France should be eaten fresh from the tree.

white with a yellow cast, crisp, firm, tender, and quite juicy. Excellent for eating fresh and for desserts and salads. Available: (32sD).

'Red June.' Origin: North Carolina. Tree is medium height, growing upright and spreading. Bears small- or below-medium-sized apples, with a deep red over yellow or greenish skin. Flesh is white, fine, and tender. Excellent eaten fresh and for desserts and salads. Available: (10), (17), (20), (24s), (32sD), (35D), (36), (39).

'Summer Rambo.' Origin: France. Probably one of the oldest varieties known. Tree is a strong grower, very vigorous and hardy, with a semispreading growth habit. Fruit is very large and flat. Skin is greenish-yellow with bright red stripes. The tender flesh is juicy. An excellent apple eaten fresh and for sauce. Available: (1s), (2s), (24s), (27s), (32sD), (36D).

'Twenty Ounce.' Origin: Massachusetts. Tree is medium-sized, growing upright, eventually becoming roundish. It is vigorous, hardy, healthy, and long-lived, but produces only moderate crops. Fruit is large to very large, as the name suggests, with green skin that becomes yellow tinged red as it matures. Flesh is white, coarse, and juicy. Very good for most culinary uses, but not a good keeper. An almost annual bearer. Available: (24s), (27s), (28s), (32sD), (48sD).

Midseason to late

'Black Gilliflower' ('Sheepnose'). Origin: Connecticut. A large, upright, spreading tree which bears medium-to-large fruit. Its dark red skin turns somewhat purple as it matures, hence the name. The flesh is whitish or slightly tinged with yellow; firm and rather coarse texture. Sometimes used for baking, it is generally considered too dry and not sour enough for cooking. A reliable annual cropper. Available: (24s), (27s), (32sD).

'Blue Pearmain.' A very large, spreading tree, with a variable bearing habit. Not a reliable cropper. Fruit is medium to very large. Skin is yellow, washed and mottled with red. Flesh is firm, rather coarse, yellow, and juicy. Good as a dessert or salad apple, or for cider. Cooking quality is only fair. Available: (2s), (32sD).

'Cox Orange.' Origin: Bucks, England. Tree is medium-sized—sometimes larger—with a dense, upright growth habit. A heavy bearer of red and yellow medium-sized fruit. Flesh is yellow, firm, crisp, and tender. Very juicy and decidedly aromatic, it is an excellent dessert apple. It also processes very well. Tree bears regularly and productively. Available: (27s), (28s), (32sD).

'Fameuse' ('Snow Apple'). Origin: France. One of the oldest apple varieties. Tree is medium in height, with an upright, spreading growth habit. A heavy bearer of light, bright red fruit. Flesh is snow-white and crisp. The aromatic, sweet taste somewhat resembles the McIntosh, of which it is an ancestor. Excellent eaten fresh and for desserts and salads, but it is not a cooking apple. A biennial to variable bearer, it grows best at high elevations in well-drained, light soil. Available: (2s), (24s), (27s), (28s), (32D).

'Hubbardston Nonesuch.' Origin: Massachusetts. Tree vigor and fruit character vary considerably with different soil and climate conditions. A heavy bearer, with an erect-to-roundish spreading growth habit. Fruit is above medium to large. Skin is yellow or greenish. Flesh is white, slightly tinged yellow, medium-firm, fine-grained, and tender. The smaller and better colored fruit will be the better keepers. As an eating apple it is acceptable but does not cook well. An annual bearer, it takes 4 to 6 years to the first crop. Available: (2s), (28s), (32sD).

'Maiden Blush.' Origin: Unknown. A medium-sized tree with an open, spreading growth habit. Fruit is medium-sized, with pale lemon-yellow skin. Flesh is white with a very slight yellow tinge, fine to moderately crisp, and tender. Very juicy, with a sprightly flavor, it is an excellent drying apple, but not a good keeper. It bears biennially, almost annually, taking 4 to 6 years for the first crop. Available: (20), (32sD).

'Porter.' Origin: Massachusetts. A compact tree with desirable growth characteristics. Fruit is usually rather large, clear, bright yellow marked with red. Flesh is white, fine, crisp, and tender. Long a favorite of home fruit growers because it retains its flavor and form well when cooked and canned. It is also fine for eating raw.

'Hubbardston Nonesuch' was once the pride of Massachusetts.

'Twenty-ounce' is one of the really big apples.

An alternate bearer, taking 4 to 6 years for the first crop. Available: (32sD).

'Westfield-Seek-No-Further.' Origin: Massachusetts. A medium-to-large, slender tree, with a spreading, roundish growth habit. Bears light crops of medium-sized, deep yellow or greenish fruit, often shaded and splashed bright pink. Flesh is slightly tinged pale yellow; firm, medium-grained, and crisp. Excellent eaten fresh and in desserts and salads, but does not cook well. Available: (27s), (28s), (32sD).

'Wolf River.' Origin: Wisconsin. A large, strong, spreading tree valued for its hardiness. Bears medium crops of very large, yellow fruit, striped red. Flesh is firm, tender, and moderately coarse. Keeping quality is very short. Fair for eating and poor for cooking. A variable bearer. Available: (2s), (24), (29), (32D).

'Yellow Bellflower.' Origin: New Jersey. Tree grows medium to large, with an upright, spreading growth habit. Bears light crops of very attractive yellow fruit with a pinkish blush that improves in storage. Flesh is white, tinged pale yellow; firm, fine-grained, and crisp. Excellent for eating fresh and for desserts and salads, it also makes very good pies. A variable bearer. Available: (10), (32sD).

Late varieties

'Arkansas Black.' Origin: Benton County, Arkansas. A large tree with an upright, spreading, moderately vigorous growth habit. Bears medium- to below-average-sized fruit. Skin is yellow covered with purplish-red. Flesh is hard and crisp, tinged yellow. Excellent for sauce. An alternate bearer, taking 8 to 10 years to the first crop. Available: (10), (11), (15), (24s), (34s).

'Baldwin Woodpecker.' Origin: Massachusetts. A very large, vigorous tree, with an upright, spreading growth habit. Bears medium-to-heavy crops of medium-sized yellow or greenish fruit, striped red. Flesh is yellow and juicy. Texture is hard and crisp. Flavor is tart and mildly acid. Excellent for freezing, and good for sauce, jam, or jelly. A biennial, and sometimes triennial, bearing habit, taking 8 to 10 years to the first crop. Available: (2s), (4D), (6), (25sD), (27s), (28s).

'Ben Davis.' Origin: Tennessee. Tree is medium height, vigorous, hardy, with an upright, spreading growth habit. Fruit is medium to large with bright red skin. The flesh is exceedingly firm, crisp, and slightly acid in flavor. Has a tendency to turn mealy when over-ripe. A good apple for drying, fair for cooking, poor for eating. Annual-bearing and exceedingly productive, taking 4 to 6 years to the first crop. Available: (24s), (31sD).

'Esopus Spitzenberg.' Origin: Ulster County, New York. Tree is a slow grower with upright, moderately drooping branches. Should be planted with ample room and pruned to allow air and light in. Fruit is medium to large, bright red, and uniform in shape. Flesh is a rich, deep yellow, covered with bright red and has a mildly acid flavor. Texture is firm, crisp, and tender. A good all-round apple, except for baking. A moderate, biennial cropper taking 6 to 8 years to the first crop. Available: (2s), (24s), (27s), (28s), (32sD).

'Golden Russet.' Origin: Unknown. Tree varies from medium to large and has an upright, roundish, spreading growth habit. Fruit is nearly round, golden russet with a bronze cheek. Flesh is yellowish, fine-grained, crisp, and tender. Excellent for eating fresh and for desserts and salads. Only fair for baking. This hardy, vigorous tree bears early, produces small aromatic fruit almost annually. Available: (23D), (27s), (28s), (32sD).

'Grimes Golden.' Origin: West Virginia. Very probably a parent of the 'Golden Delicious.' Tree is medium to large, with a dense, spreading growth habit. Fruit has a golden yellow skin and yellow, tender, crisp, juicy flesh. Bears small fruit that is very good for eating and freezing, but poor for baking. An intermediate bearer, taking 6 to 8 years to the first crop. Widely available.

Apple families

We mentioned earlier that some apples are the heads of extensive families, varying in some detail of color or growth habit. These apple families come about in two ways: they are the result of breeding; or they are sports (natural genetic changes) of the original tree.

Sports may occur at any time. Often there is no apparent reason for them—suddenly one branch of a tree is different. Occasionally the odd branch results from mechanical damage, such as pruning. Sometimes experimenters purposely change genetic structure with chemicals or radiation. Most sports are without value, but some are valuable and are propagated to create new strains.

In breeding, each parent supplies half the heritage of the seedlings, but that half may be a set of characteristics that is partly or completely hidden in the parent. The seedlings are a mixed bag, and breeders must grow them to fruiting size to see what they have, so the work takes time and the seedlings may be inferior trees.

'Delicious.' The best known modern apple sprouted in an Iowa orchard in 1870. The owner, Jesse Hiatt, cut it down twice, but it resprouted, and finally he let it grow. It seemed to be a seedling of the Bellflower tree next to it. In about 1880 it bore fruit which Hiatt thought was the best he had ever tasted. The name 'Delicious' was given at a fruit show by C. M. Stark of Stark Nurseries. Stark didn't learn the name of the grower until 1894, but then 'Delicious' began its rise to fame.

Redder-colored sports include: 'Richard,' 'Royal Red,' 'Hi Early,' 'Chelan Red,' 'Red Queen,' and others. The original red sport was 'Starking.' Spur-type sports include: 'Starkrimson,' 'Redspur,' 'Wellspur,' 'Hardispur,' and 'Oregon Spur.' 'Delicious' is a parent of 'Melrose.'

'Jonathan.' The seedling sprouted in Kingston, N.Y., apparently from a fruit of an 'Esopus Spitzenberg.' A Judge Buel of Albany found the apple so good that he presented specimens to the Massachusetts Horticultural Society, giving it the name 'Jonathan' for the man who first showed it to him. 'Jonathan' was the primary variety before 'Delicious' took over.

Red sports of 'Jonathan' include 'Jon-A-Red,' and 'Jonnee.' Hybrid descendants include: 'Jonagold,' 'Jonamac,' 'Ida-red,' 'Melrose,' 'Minjon,' and 'Monroe.'

'McIntosh.' The apple came from the McIntosh Nursery in Ontario, Canada. John McIntosh discovered it about 1811, but did not propagate grafted stock until 1835 when the grafting technique was perfected. 'McIntosh' became widely known in about 1900.

A well-known spur variety is 'Macspur.' 'McIntosh' is frequently used in breeding, and well-known descendants include: 'Summerred,' 'Niagara,' 'Early McIntosh,' 'Puritan,' 'Tydeman's Red,' 'Jonamac,' 'Macoun,' 'Empire,' 'Cortland,' and 'Spartan.'

Other major apples with crowds of offspring include, 'Rome,' 'Golden Delicious,' 'Northern Spy,' and 'Winesap.'

'Hunt Russet' (Russet Pearmain'). Origin: Massachusetts. Tree is medium height, upright, and spreading. Fruit is medium-sized, golden russet with a red-russet cheek. Rather fine, tender flesh is whitish tinged yellow. Flavor is mild to bland. Good eaten fresh or for sauces, pies, jams, jellies, cider, or juice. A variable bearing habit. Available: (32sD).

'Lady.' Origin: France. Tree grows somewhat dwarfish. Fruit is small, with exquisite red and green coloring. Highly decorative, it is often used at Christmas time. Flesh is white, crisp, and firm. Its flavor is subacid, turning to very sweet. Excellent for a fresh dessert and also makes very good juice and cider. This is a very old variety, grown and enjoyed almost back to the Middle Ages. A biennial bearer. Available: (2s), (28s), (32sD).

'Northern Spy.' Origin: East Bloomfield, New York. Tree is medium to large. Bears large, roundish, bright red, striped fruit. Flesh is yellowish, firm, fine-grained, tender, and juicy. Still the standard for excellence in cooking and processing. It is an intermediate bearer, taking 10 to 14 years to the first crop. Tree is resistant to cedar rust. Widely available.

'Pumpkin Sweet' ('Pound Sweet'). Origin: Manchester, Connecticut. Tree is medium to large, with an upright, spreading growth habit. A reliable cropper of large to very large fruit. Skin color is first green—then turns clear yellow with greenish-yellow stripes. Flesh is yellow and has a peculiar, sweet flavor. Excellent for baking; poor for eating. Tree bears alternately, taking 6 to 8 years to the first crop. Plant in a wind-sheltered area as fruit is subject to windfall. Available: (2s), (32sD).

'Roxbury Russet.' Origin: Massachusetts. The most popular of the Russets. Tree is medium to large, with a spreading, flat growth habit. Fruit is above medium to large, greenish- to yellowish-brown. Flesh is tinged with yellow, and is firm, coarse, and juicy. A good apple for cellar storage and a favorite for blending in cider. Bears annually. Available: (2s), (28s), (32sD).

'Smokehouse.' Origin: Lancaster County, Pennsylvania. Large, dense, roundish trees bear above-medium-to-large fruit. Skin is yellow or greenish, mottled dull red. Flesh is tinged yellow, rather firm, and delicately aromatic. Good for eating fresh and for desserts and salads. A reliable bearer. Available: (1s), (24s), (27s), (32sD).

'Tolman Sweet.' Origin: Dorchester, Massachusetts. Tree is very hardy, long-lived, grows well, bears early and almost annually. Fruit is medium to large with a pale, clear yellow skin and firm white flesh. Flavor is rather dry and decidedly sweet. An excellent eating and baking apple. Keeping quality is short. Fruit is easily damaged so should be handled with care. A biennial bearer. Available: (23D), (28s), (32sD).

'White Pearmain.' Origin: Unknown. Large trees bear heavy crops of small to fairly large fruit. Skin is greenish to pale yellow shaded with brownish red. Flesh is white tinged yellow, fine-grained, crisp, tender, and firm. A juicy, pleasantly aromatic apple that is excellent eaten fresh and in desserts, salads, and pies. Also good for sauce, jam, jelly, cider, and juice. Keeping quality is very good. An annual bearer, taking 6 to 8 years to the first crop. Available: (10), (32sD).

In addition to the above, these old apple varieties are listed by the following sources:
'Gold Pearmain' (25)
'Red Pearmain' (32)
'Yellow Horse' (1)

'Rome Beauty' is a beauty, but not the best of the eating apples. Use it for splendid baked apples.

Pears

Pears, and especially dwarf pears, are a fine choice for the home gardener. The trees are attractive even in winter, they require little pruning after they begin to bear, and the fruit stores fairly well without special apparatus. The plants take well to formal or informal training, so space is no problem.

The one real drawback with pears is fire blight, but a home gardener can work around it by a wise choice of variety, or by replacement of plants if it comes to that. Dwarf pears come into bearing fairly quickly. Fire blight is at its worst in spring when insects carry it from tree to tree. Resistant plants are the best answer. Cut off any infected tissue well below the infection and burn it.

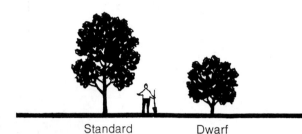

Standard   Dwarf

The size of the tree

Standard pears will spread 25 feet across and grow as tall or taller. A dwarf in natural shape needs about 15 square feet of space, but with the training methods listed under Space-Saver Training (page 79) you can grow a pear flat against a fence or wall, using next to no space. The silhouettes let you compare naturally shaped trees.

Small-space planting

A pear is as trainable as an apple, and where fire blight can be controlled, a trained tree can last 75 years. Plant pears as espaliers, train them to 45-degree angles for an informal hedge, or try them in tubs as a single cordon or on a trellis.

In the ground, use grafting or two-in-one-hole planting to save space with naturally shaped trees.

Where does the fruit grow?

Pears bear on long-lived spurs, much as apples do. (See the sketch of apple spurs on page 23.) These spurs last a long time if you're careful not to damage them when picking.

Pruning pears

Train naturally shaped trees to three or four main scaffolds and then trim away tangles. Once the tree bears, prune very lightly except when a branch is blighted. Remove a sick branch well below the infection and paint the wound with a product containing fixed copper.

Thinning the fruit

You don't need to thin, but if a very heavy crop sets, remove fruit that is damaged or very undersized. Thin a few weeks before harvest.

Pollination

All pears can be considered to need a pollinator. Use almost any other pear. Bartlett is a poor pollinator for Seckel.

Pests and disease

Fire blight is the major difficulty. Other pests are codling moth and pear slug. See the page on Pests and Disease, beginning page 74.

Pear harvesting

Most fruits are best when picked ripe or nearly so. Pears are the exception. A tree-ripe pear breaks down and turns soft and brown at the core. Always harvest pears when they have reached full size but are still green and very firm. Hold them in a cool, dark place if you intend to eat them

'Seckel' is small and no beauty, but you won't find a finer aroma or flavor, for eating or cooking.

within a few weeks. For longer storage, refrigerate the harvested fruit, then remove it from cold storage about a week before you want to use it. Pears ripen faster if they are held with other pears in a poorly ventilated spot. For fast ripening, place several in a plastic bag together.

The variety list

Catalog numbers at the end of each entry include a small "s" where semi-dwarf trees are sold, and a "D" for dwarf trees.

Early midseason

'Clapp's Favorite.' A large yellow fruit with red cheek, resembling Bartlett. The flesh is soft and sweet, good both for eating and canning. The tree is of attractive shape and very productive, but highly susceptible to fire blight. Since it is very hardy, the variety is best in cold, late-spring zones. Available: (1), (2D), (4D), (6D), (14D), (23D), (25sD), (27D), (31D), (32D), (44sD).

'Moonglow.' Origin: Beltsville, MD. The large and attractive fruit is soft and juicy, nearly free of grit. The flavor is mild. Use it for canning or eating fresh. The very upright and vigorous tree is heavily spurred and begins bearing a good crop very young. It is resistant to fire blight, so use it where the disease is a severe problem. Available: (1), (2D), (4), (6), (8D), (10), (11), (14D), (18), (20), (27D), (32D), (34D), (44sD).

Midseason

'Bartlett.' The medium-to-large, thin-skinned yellow fruit is familiar to most people, since this is a major commercial pear. The flesh is very sweet and tender, fine for eating, but a good canner too. The tree form is not especially good, and the variety is subject to fire blight. It takes summer heat, provided there is adequate cold in winter. In cool climates it sets poorly without a pollinator (use any variety but 'Seckel'). This widely available pear is sold by most of our sources.

'Lincoln.' Called by some "The most dependable pear for the Midwest," the variety bears large fruits abundantly every year. The tree is extremely hardy and blight resistant. Available: (13), (17).

'Maxine' ('Starking Delicious'). Origin: Miami County, OH. The large and attractive fruit has firm, white flesh that is juicy and sweet. The tree is somewhat blight-resistant. Available: (13), (17), (20D), (27D), (32D), (40).

'Parker.' Origin: Excelsior, MN. The medium-to-large fruit is yellow with a red blush. The flesh is white, juicy, pleasantly sweet. The upright and vigorous tree is fairly hardy but susceptible to fire blight. Available: (12), (22), (29).

Late midseason

'Anjou.' A French pear from the mild area near the Loire. The fruit is large and green with a stocky neck. The flesh is of a rather mild flavor, not especially juicy, but firm. Use it for eating or canning. It stores well. The upright and vigorous tree is susceptible to fire blight. Not a tree for hot-summer areas. Available: (1), (2), (7), (10s), (14D), (19), (25sD), (27D), (33D), (34D), (35s), (38D), (44sD), (45), (46D).

'Bosc.' A French pear. The long, narrow fruit is heavily russeted. The flesh is firm, even crisp, with a heavy perfume that makes some people consider it among the very finest pears. Good fresh or canned. A fine cooking pear as well. The very large tree is highly susceptible to fire blight. Don't place the fruit in cold storage. Available: (1), (2), (7), (10), (14D), (19), (23), (25sD), (32), (34), (35), (44sD).

A mixed harvest, including tiny 'Old Home,' a rootstock variety.

'Bartlett.' Green at left. Pick it like this, but eat it when it resembles center fruit. At right it's too ripe.

'Duchess.' A French pear. The fruit is very large and greenish-yellow. The flesh is buttery, melting, and of fine flavor. The tree is symmetrical, bears early and annually. Available: (2), (4), (13D), (17D), (20D), (23D), (25sD), (34D).

'Gorham.' Origin: Geneva, NY. The fruit is of excellent quality, strongly resembling 'Bartlett' but ripening later and can be stored longer. The dense and upright tree is vigorous and productive. Available: (28D), (32D).

'Patten.' Origin: Charles City, IA. The large and juicy fruit is particularly good fresh, fair for canning. Since the tree is especially hardy, the variety should be considered for the northern Mississippi Valley where 'Bartlett' and 'Anjou' fail. Available: (12).

'Seckel.' A small, yellow-brown fruit that is not especially attractive, but has the finest aroma and flavor of any home garden pear. Eat it fresh or use the small fruit whole for spiced preserves. The highly productive tree is very fire blight-resistant, but sets fruit best with a pollinator (not 'Bartlett'). Available: (1), (2D), (6D), (7), (10), (13), (14D), (20D), (23), (24), (25sD), (26D), (27D), (31D), (32D), (34D), (35), (36D), (40D), (44sD).

Late season

'Dumont.' European origin. A large pear with blushed yellow skin. The flesh is firm and juicy with a sweet, rich flavor. One of the best winter pears. The tree tends to alternate bearing, especially as it grows old. Available: (28D), (32D).

'Winter Nelis.' The fruit is small and rounded, green to yellow-green and russeted, rather unattractive, but of good flavor and it keeps well. The fairly vigorous tree is not very susceptible to fire blight. It is a good variety for hot-summer areas if there is enough winter cold. You must plant a pollinator. Available: (10s), (38), (45), (46D).

Peaches

The peach is rightly one of the most popular of home-grown fruits. Both peaches and their fuzzless sisters, the nectarines, are at their best when tree-ripened, so a home gardener's time and trouble with pruning shears and spray tank are rewarded by a product that money can't buy.

But should you grow peaches at all? Consider the following to make your decision: Peaches cannot tolerate extreme winter cold nor late frost, so in the northern Plains states and northern New England peaches are pure experiment. The hardiest, such as 'Reliance,' may survive and bear in a protected spot, but you can't be sure. In more temperate climates near the Great Lakes peaches do well, but choose the warmest site available for planting. A protected, sunny spot where cold air can't collect and sit is the right place for your tree.

The size of the tree

The silhouettes here can tell you a lot about what to expect from a young nursery tree. The standard peach grows 15 to 18 feet tall and about as wide. Your pruning holds

Standard   Semidwarf   Genetic dwarf

it at that size. A semidwarf tree on Nanking cherry or St. Julien plum rootstock stays at seven to nine feet tall and also requires pruning to maintain it and to encourage new fruiting wood. The true, or genetic, dwarf peaches grow in bush shape to four to six feet tall and need next to no pruning, but they won't stand really hard winters. Try them in a container that can be wheeled into a shelter for the winter.

Small-space planting

You can fit a peach into whatever space is available to you, although it won't take the formal training that you can practice with an apple. Among commercial growers these days there is a trend to the hedgerow, a narrow wall of trees formed by training young plants to a V-shaped scaffold, then pruning to hold all growth within the hedge shape. See page 82 for a trellis version of the V-scaffold.

Semidwarf peaches are ideal for hedge training and they lend themselves well to another simple technique that is the home gardener's specialty. Dig an extra big planting hole and set two to four varieties together with their roots almost touching. You'll get the effect of a single small tree with several kinds of fruit. Of course you can do the same with standard trees.

The genetic dwarfs are great for patio container plantings. Protect them in winter, but wheel them out on mild spring days for insect pollination of the bloom. You may still need night protection in regions with late frost.

Where does the fruit grow?

The sketch on page 35 will show you the most important thing about a peach tree. It illustrates where on the branch you'll find flowers and fruit. Notice that fruit is formed only on branch segments that grew the previous summer. New

Many fruiting peaches have large, showy flowers.

wood grows on beyond the fruit and will produce next year's crop. Once fruit is harvested, the section of branch on which it grew will never fruit again. That's why you need to encourage new growth for replacement branches.

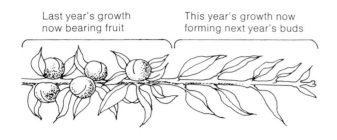

Last year's growth now bearing fruit   This year's growth now forming next year's buds

Pruning a peach
How do you encourage new growth on your standard or semidwarf trees? Pruning does it. You thin, head back, and remove weak branches. The tree responds with lush growth. See page 94 for details and a sketch of cuts to make.

Thinning the fruit
Once a crop sets on a peach tree, you may not even see the branch through the fruit. You can't leave it all for three reasons: It will be too small; it slows branch growth and cuts next year's crop; and it may snap branches. Thin it out when it reaches thumbnail size. For an early peach, leave six to eight inches of space between each fruit. For a late peach, thin after June fruit fall and leave four to five inches between each fruit. If a frost knocked off a lot of your crop, leave all the rest, even if they're clustered. The important thing is the ratio of leaf surface to number of peaches, so a sparse crop will do fine even in bunches.

Special advice
Peaches are twiggy trees, but the greatest number of flower buds form on sturdy new branches that made more than 10 inches of growth the previous summer. Keep these and thin the more anemic twigs. You can head the strong ones back by a third to a half if you want to keep the tree small. They'll bloom on the remaining half.

Pollination
Only a few peach varieties need a pollinator ('J. H. Hale' is one of the best known). Normally the trees are self-fertile, although bees are a big help in pollen transfer.

Winter chill
Any peach needs cold weather in winter, but some varieties have been bred for short, mild winters and may bloom too early or freeze in the North. Be sure to buy hardy, high-chill varieties.

Pests and disease
Brown rot and plum curculio are the chief pests. Look for control methods on page 74 to 77. Other common troubles: leaf curl, peach tree borer.

The variety list
These are the best choices for Northern gardens.

The "s" and "D" after catalog numbers mean semidwarf and dwarf are available.

Early
'Garnet Beauty.' Origin: Ontario, Canada. An early sport of Redhaven. Medium-large, semifreestone fruit, hangs on tree until overripe. Flesh is yellow, streaked with red, firm, slightly fibrous texture, melting. Tree is very vigorous,

hardy. Produces heavy crops which size and color well even inside the tree. Susceptible to bacterial spot. Widely available.

'Golden Jubilee.' Origin: New Jersey A.E.S. An old standby. Widely available. Medium-large freestone. Skin mottled bright red. Flesh yellow, firm, coarse texture. Sets heavy but is self-thinning. Tree very hardy. Widely available.

'Harbelle.' Origin: Ontario, Canada Agr. Res. Sta. Medium-sized freestone. Skin red blush over yellow ground. Flesh yellow, firm, melting. Needs thinning. Tree compact, moderately vigorous, moderately productive. Tolerates bacterial spot. Widely available.

'Ranger.' Origin: Maryland USDA. Medium-large freestone. Skin red mottled over greenish-yellow to yellow-gold ground color. Flesh yellow, flecked with red, firm, medium to fine textured, melting. Tree moderately vigorous, consistently productive. Good resistance to bacterial rot. Cans and freezes well. Available: (2), (10s), (11), (18), (45).

'Redhaven.' Origin: Michigan A.E.S. Medium-sized freestone. Widely recommended and widely available. One of the finest early peaches. Skin deep red over yellow ground. Flesh yellow, firm, melting, nonbrowning. Fruit sets heavily, thin, is good for freezing. Tree is spreading, vigorous, highly productive. Resistance to bacteriosis.

'Reliance.' Origin: New Hampshire A.E.S. Promising home garden variety. Very winter hardy. Will withstand —20 to —25°F. during January and February and still produce a crop that same year. Large freestone. Skin dark red over yellow ground. Flesh bright yellow, medium firm, slightly stringy. Showy flowers. Widely available.

'Sunhaven.' Origin: Michigan A.E.S. Medium-large freestone. Skin bright red over golden ground. Short, soft fuzz. Flesh yellow flecked with red, firm, fine textured, nonbrowning. Vigorous, consistently productive. Widely available.

Midseason
'Glohaven.' Origin: Michigan A.E.S. Large freestone. Skin red over deep yellow. Flesh yellow, firm, nonbrowning. Flowers medium-sized deep pink. Tree vigorous, hardy. Cans, freezes well. Fruit remains on tree when mature. Widely available.

'Halehaven.' Origin: Michigan A.E.S. Widely available. Medium-large freestone. Skin dark red over yellow ground. Flesh yellow, firm, melting. Tree vigorous, productive. Susceptible to brown rot. Widely available.

'Jerseyland.' Origin: New Jersey A.E.S. Large semifreestone. Skin dark red over greenish-yellow ground. Flesh yellow, melting. Tree vigorous, productive. Available: (2), (11), (18), (36).

'J. H. Hale.' Extra-large freestone. Skin deep crimson over yellow ground. Skin nearly fuzzless. Flesh golden yellow, firm. Needs cross-pollination for best production. Widely available.

'Loring.' Origin: Missouri A.E.S. Medium-sized freestone. Skin blushed red over yellow ground. Slight fuzz. Flesh yellow, firm, medium texture, melting. Dependable cropper and sets fruit under adverse weather conditions. Tolerant to bacteriosis. Widely available.

'Raritan Rose.' Origin: New Jersey A.E.S. Medium-large freestone. Skin red, over yellow ground. Flesh white, streaked red, fine-textured, melting, watery. Flowers showy. Tree spreading, vigorous, hardy, productive. Tolerant to bacteriosis. Available: (1), (28D), (44sD).

'Trioqem.' Origin: New Jersey A.E.S. Sets heavily and produces crops under adverse weather conditions. Medium-sized freestone. Skin dull red over yellow ground. Flesh yellow streaked with red, firm, melting. Thin early and heavy. Ripens slowly. Good for canning. Available: (1), (2), (11), (18), (28D), (48).

Late

'Blake.' Origin: New Jersey A.E.S. Large freestone. Skin red, slight fuzziness. Flesh yellow, firm, melting. Fruit hangs well on tree. Tree vigorous, productive, but sometimes erratic. Good freezing, excellent canning. Susceptible to bacteriosis. Available: (1), (2), (11), (18), (23), (36), (44sD).

'Cresthaven.' Origin: Michigan A.E.S. Medium-large freestone. Skin bright red over gold ground. Almost fuzzless. Flesh yellow nonbrowning. Tree hardy. Fruit remains on tree when mature. Good canning and freezing. Widely available.

'Elberta.' The old standard bearer for a midseason crop. Large freestone. Skin red blushed over a deep golden yellow ground color. Fruit tends to drop at maturity. Slight bitterness around pit is preferred by many. Resistance to brown rot. Widely available.

'Georgia Belle.' Origin: Georgia USDA. Outstanding white peach. Skin red blushed over creamy white. Flesh white, firm. Tree vigorous, hardy, productive. Very susceptible to brown rot. Excellent eating. Fair freezing. Poor canner. Widely available.

'Jefferson.' Origin: Virginia A.E.S. Especially suited to localities where late spring frosts are a problem. Noted for fine texture and flavor. Skin bright red over bright orange ground. Flesh yellow, firm. Reliable production. Cans and freezes well. Some tolerance to brown rot. Widely available.

'Jerseyqueen.' Origin: New Jersey A.E.S. Large freestone. Bright red over yellow ground. Flesh yellow, firm. Flowers showy. Tree productive. Widely available.

'Madison.' Origin: Virginia A.E.S. Adapted to mountain area of Virginia. Exceptional tolerance to frosts during blossoming season. Sets crops where others fail. Medium-sized freestone. Skin bright red over bright orange-yellow ground color. Flesh orange-yellow, very firm, fine texture. Tree average-vigorous. Widely available.

'Monroe.' Origin: Virginia A.E.S. Large stone. Skin red over orange-yellow ground. Flesh yellow-orange, firm, fine texture. Flowers showy, pink. Tree moderately productive. Reliable producer. Good in its season. Above-average tolerance to blossoming season frost. Disease-tolerant. Available: (2), (11), (18), (34), (36).

'Sunhigh.' Origin: New Jersey A.E.S. Very good in its season. Medium-large freestone. Skin bright red over yellow ground. Flesh yellow, firm. Tree vigorous, spreading. Very susceptible to bacteriosis. Requires thorough summer spraying. Widely available.

Nectarines

These fuzzless peach sports are very sensitive to brown rot.

Early

'Nectared 1.' Origin: New Jersey A.E.C. Attractive, smooth-finished, yellow flesh. Large semifreestone. Blushed red over yellow ground. Tree is moderately productive. Available: (14D), (18), (44sD).

'Pocohontas.' Origin: Virginia A.E.S. One of the best early yellow-fleshed nectarines. Medium-large semifreestone is highly colored. Flesh is slightly stringy. Tree vigorous.

'Early Elberta' resembles namesake, ripens a week sooner. Choose an early white peach for mild climates.

Flowers showy. Escapes damage to brown rot and frost during blossoming season. Available: (2), (8), (14D), (18), (28), (36).

Midseason

'Cherokee.' Origin: Virginia A.E.S. Widely recommended, above-average quality, rich-flavored medium-large semi-freestone. Highly colored with fine finish. Tree moderately vigorous, productive. Flowers showy. Above-average tolerance to brown rot infection and spring frost. Available: (2), (14).

'Garden State.' Origin: New Jersey A.E.S. Juicy, firm, yellow-fleshed large freestone with red blush over greenish-yellow ground. Tree vigorous, productive, medium-sized and spreading. Flowers showy, light pink. Available: (2D), (7), (8D), (35D).

'Lafayette.' Origin: Virginia Polytechnic Institute. Another white-fleshed freestone with bright red, smooth finished skin color. Good crops borne annually. Heavy producer of fruit on tree of average vigor and above average hardiness. Flowers showy. Available: (2), (36).

'Lexington.' Widely recommended. Very hardy. Slightly larger than Cavalier which it resembles. Medium-large freestone. Skin medium red blush over deep yellow ground. Flesh deep yellow, medium-firm. Tree very vigorous. Flowers showy. Good ability to escape brown rot and blossom-season frost. Available: (18), (28), (36).

'Nectared 4.' Origin: New Jersey A.E.S. Medium-large semifreestone. Skin red blush over yellow ground, smooth. Flesh yellow. Tree productive. Flowers showy. Available: (14D), (18), (44sD).

'Redbud.' Origin: Virginia A.E.S. White-fleshed, bright red freestone with smooth finish. Fruit is medium sized. Tree moderately vigorous. Sets heavily. Flowers showy. Has good ability to escape brown rot infection and blossom-season frost damage. Available: (36).

'Sunglo.' Origin: California. One of the highest quality nectarines. Heavy bearing. Requires heavy thinning and extra nitrogen for best performance. Medium-sized freestone. Skin bright red over golden orange. Flesh is firm, melting. Available: (34D).

Late

'Cavalier.' Origin: Virginia A.E.S. Resembles 'Garden State.' Attractive medium-large freestone with good finish. Skin dark red mottled over orange-yellow ground. Flesh yellow and firm. Slightly bitter but quality better than average. Tree is vigorous, hardy, productive. Sets fruit buds heavily which are very tolerant of spring frosts. Flowers are showy. Reported resistance to brown rot. Available: (2), (18), (36).

Genetic dwarf peaches

Only the hardiest can go in the ground. Use them in containers.

'Bonanza.' Origin: California. This is one of the oldest, widely known dwarfs. The medium-sized fruit has a moderately red skin. The freestone flesh is yellow and ripens early. The tree needs moderate winter chill. The showy flowers are pink and semidouble. Available: (14), (23), (46).

'Compact Redhaven.' Origin: Orondo, WA. Not the same background as other dwarfs. This peach is a chance sport that is like 'Redhaven' in everything but size. It grows with leaf nodes close together to about 10 feet tall. Will take more cold than other dwarfs, and grows where 'Redhaven' grows. Available: (22), (34).

Choose a low-chill peach for warm winters.
Genetic dwarf 'Bonanza' bears full-sized fruit.

Spray for brown rot as fruit ripens.

Plums

Of all the stone fruits, plums are the most varied, from hardy little cherry plums and sand cherries, to hybrids with the hardiness of natives, to European-type plums. In the milder regions, particularly along the Eastern seaboard, some Japanese-type plums are also grown. Plums go on bearing for 10 to 15 years and sometimes more.

The size of the tree
Check the silhouettes here for size comparison. Standard trees take space. Count on your tree filling an area 20 by

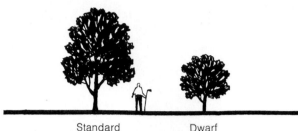

Standard   Dwarf

20 feet. Bush and cherry plums can be used in smaller spaces and reach six feet or so, but may spread as wide or wider. A dwarfed European plum on Nanking cherry roots will reach 10 or 12 feet in height.

Where is the fruit?
Plums bear on spurs along the older branches with the heaviest production on wood that is from two to four years old.

Check the variety list for pollinators. Most plums need a pollinator, although European kinds are partly or entirely self-fertile.

Typical European plum; note the egg shape.

Pruning and thinning for good crops
Plums need little or no thinning except for the large-fruited Japanese kinds. The young trees should be trained as discussed on page 91. Bush varieties need their oldest shoots trimmed off at ground level after about four years of bearing to encourage new growth.

Japanese plums overgrow and overbear. Cut back the long whips as discussed under Apricots on page 94, and thin fruit at thumbnail size, leaving four to six inches between remaining fruits.

Space-saver planting
Tree plums don't lend themselves to confinement, but you can plant several to one hole for pollinization and a choice of fruit. Use bush types as shrubby screens or try them in containers.

Pests and disease
Brown rot is a major concern and means summer spraying. See details on page 76.

The variety list

Check for hardiness and pollinizing requirements. The "s" and "D" after catalog numbers mean semi-dwarf or dwarf trees are sold.

European plums

The fruit tends to be small, and most varieties are egg-shaped. The flesh is rather dry and very sweet. Prunes are the sweetest, easiest to dry. The plants are fairly hardy but do well where winter is mild.

Early
'Earliblue.' (Best: North.) The blue fruit has tender, green-yellow flesh, resembling 'Stanley' but softer.

Plum blossoms make spring show.

Blue is the most common European plum color.

The tree is hardy but bears late. Production is moderate, but fine for the home garden. Pollinator: 'Mohawk.' Ripens: mid- to late July in Michigan. Available: (34), (44).

Midseason

'Green Gage' ('Reine Claude'). (Best: any region.) Old European variety. The greenish-yellow fruit has amber flesh and is good fresh, cooked, or preserved. Trees are medium-sized. Pollinator: self. Ripens: mid-July, later North. Available: wide distribution.

'German Prune.' (Best: New York.) Very old European variety. A purple freestone with amber flesh. The fruit ripens over a very long period. Pollinator: self. Ripens: August. Available: (10), (25sD).

'Mohawk.' (Best: North.) Origin: New York. A large, blue, prune-type fruit for fresh use or for cooking. Pollinator: any European. Ripens: early to mid-August. Available: (28).

'Mount Royal.' (Best: North.) The deep blue fruit is freestone. The tree is among the hardiest and stands all but the most severe northern winters. Pollinator: 'Stanley.' Ripens: late August. Available: (12), (20), (22), (29).

'Stanley.' (Best: North, South.) Origin: New York. The most widely planted European plum in the East, Midwest, and South. The large, dark blue fruit has firm, richly flavored yellow flesh. The trees bear heavily every year. Hardy into central Iowa. Pollinator: self. Ripens: after mid-August, into September in northern regions. Available: wide distribution.

'Sugar.' (Best: West.) A very sweet, dark blue fruit, fairly large and excellent for home drying and canning. The trees bear in alternate years with light crops in off year. Pollinator: self. Ripens: after July 15. Available (10), (45), (46).

'Yellow Egg.' (Best: West, South.) The golden yellow fruit has a thick skin and yellow flesh. The round-topped, vigorous tree is hardy and productive. In the West, the fruit is planted in Washington. Pollinator: self. Ripens: late August. Available: (2), (35).

Late

'Bluefre.' (Best: North.) The large, blue freestone has yellow flesh. The trees are vigorous, bear young, and fruit hangs on well after ripening. Some sensitivity to brown rot. Pollinator: self. Ripens: September 1. Available: (7), (34), (44sD).

'Damson.' (Best: any region.) An old plum from Europe that is included in a different species than other European plums. The smallish blue fruits are best for jam, jelly, and preserves. There are several improved varieties, such as 'Blue Damson,' 'French Damson' (large), and 'Shropshire Damson.' The trees are small. Pollinator: self. Ripens: end of August or September. Available: wide distribution.

'Imperial Epineuse.' (Best: North.) A French variety. The large reddish-purple fruit has greenish-yellow flesh, is good fresh and excellent for canning or drying. Pollinator: 'French Prune' or other late Europeans. Ripens: early to mid-September. Available: (32).

'President.' (Best: any region.) The large, dark blue fruit has amber flesh and does not have outstanding flavor, but it ripens very late, after other plums. Use it for winter cooking or canning. Pollinator: another late European. Ripens: end of September in Michigan. Available: (1), (15), (35), (44sD), (45).

Japanese (Oriental) plums

The fruit is relatively large, soft, and juicy. The plants are the least hardy of the various kinds of plum, although selected varieties are grown in the milder northern regions.

Early

'Beauty.' (Best: California.) Origin: California (Luther Burbank). The medium-to-large fruit is bright red, and the amber flesh is tinged red. Use it fresh or cooked. The tree is strong and vigorous. Pollinator: self or 'Santa Rosa.' Ripens: early June in California. Available: (4D), (6D), (25sD), (36D), (44sD).

'Bruce.' (Best: South, Southwest.) Origin: Donley County, TX. The large fruits have red skin and red flesh. The flavor is good. The fruit matures early. The tree bears young and heavily. Pollinator: 'Santa Rosa.' Ripens: June. Available: (10), (14), (45).

'Early Golden.' (Best: North.) Origin: Canada. The medium-sized round fruit is yellow, and of fair quality. The stone is small and free. The tree is very vigorous, outgrowing other varieties, but it has a tendency to bear in alternate years. Thin carefully. Pollinator: 'Shiro,' 'Burbank.' Ripens: mid-July in Michigan. Available: (28), (39).

'Santa Rosa.' (Best: any region.) Origin: Santa Rosa, CA (Luther Burbank). Widely popular large plum with a deep crimson skin and flesh that is purplish near skin and yellow, streaked pink near pit. For dessert or canning. Pollinator: self or any early or midseason plum. Ripens: California: mid-June; North: late July. Available: wide distribution.

Oriental plums are larger, juicier, tend to red tones.

Early midseason

'Abundance.' (Best: North.) Origin: CA (Luther Burbank). The fruit is red-purple with yellow flesh. It is tender and softens quickly. For dessert or cooking. The tree tends strongly to bear every other year. Pollinator: 'Methley,' 'Shiro.' Ripens: late July in Michigan. Available: (4D), (6D), (25sD), (36D), (44sD).

'Methley.' (Best: North, South.) The small-to-medium fruit is reddish-purple with red flesh and excellent flavor. It ripens over a long period, needing several pickings. The tree is upright with hardy flower buds. Pollinator: self, 'Shiro,' 'Burbank.' Ripens: mid-July in Michigan; earlier, South. Available: wide distribution.

'Satsuma.' (Best: California, South.) Origin: California (Luther Burbank). A blood plum with red juice. The meaty fruit is small to medium with a dull, dark red skin, red flesh, and small pit. Flavor is mild and good. Use for dessert or preserves. Pollinator: 'Santa Rosa,' 'Wickson.' Ripens: after 'Santa Rosa.' Available: wide distribution.

'Shiro.' (Best: any region.) The medium-to-large fruit is round and yellow, of good flavor. The tree produces heavily. Use it fresh or for cooking. Pollinator: 'Early Golden,' 'Methley,' 'Santa Rosa.' Ripens: with 'Abundance' in Michigan; early July, California and South. Available: (1), (2D), (10), (14D), (23), (28), (44sD).

'Wickson.' (Best: California.) The large and showy yellow fruit turns reddish when ripe. The flesh is firm and of good flavor. Keeps well, good in cooking. Pollinator: 'Beauty,' 'Santa Rosa.' Ripens: late July. Available: (10), (15), (45).

Midseason

'Burbank.' (Best: any region.) Origin: Santa Rosa, CA (Luther Burbank). The large red fruit has amber flesh of excellent flavor. The trees are fairly small and somewhat drooping. Use the fruit for canning or dessert. Pollinator: 'Early Golden,' 'Santa Rosa.' Ripens: early August in Michigan; mid-July in West and South. Available: wide distribution.

'Duarte.' (Best: California.) The medium-to-large, dull red fruit has silvery markings. The flesh is deep red. Fruit keeps well, is tart when cooked. Pollinator: 'Santa Rosa,' 'Satsuma.' Ripens: late July. Available: (7), (10), (35D).

'Eldorado.' (Best: California.) Origin: California (Luther Burbank). The medium-large fruit has very dark skin and firm, rather dry, amber flesh. It holds its shape well for canning or slicing into pie. Pollinator: 'Santa Rosa,' 'Wickson.' Ripens: late July. Available: (15), (38D).

'Formosa.' (Best: California, North.) Fruit is early in California. The large fruit is greenish-yellow overlaid with red. The flesh is cream-colored, firm and juicy with a somewhat clinging pit. The tree tends to bear in alternate years. Pollinator: 'Santa Rosa,' 'Wickson.' Ripens: June in California; early August in New York, Michigan. Available: (1), (28).

'Frontier.' (Best: California, North.) Origin: Fresno, CA. The fruit is a large, blue-black freestone with red flesh. The tree is vigorous. Pollinator: 'Burbank,' 'Santa Rosa.' Ripens: about July 1 in California; mid-August in Michigan. Available: (39), (45).

'Howard Miracle.' (Best: California.) Origin: Montebello, CA. The fruit is yellow with a heavy red blush when ripe. The flesh is yellow with a distinctive, very good flavor,

A hybrid, 'Ozark Premier' bears Oriental-type fruit.

recalling pineapple. Rather acid plum. The tree is very vigorous. Pollinator: self. Ripens: after July 15. Available: (10), (45), (46D).

'Laroda.' (Best: California.) Origin: Winters, CA. The large, round fruit is deep reddish-purple with light amber flesh, reddish near the skin. The tree is vigorous with numerous spurs. Pollinator: 'Santa Rosa.' Ripens: after July 15. Available: (15), (19), (32), (35), (38D), (45).

'Mariposa.' (Best: California.) Origin: Pasadena, CA. (Also called 'Improved Satsuma.') The large round fruit has maroon skin and flesh. The tree is medium to large and needs little winter chill. A good Southern California choice. Pollinator: 'Santa Rosa,' 'Late Santa Rosa.' Ripens: mid-July. Available: (10), (38D), (45).

'Nubiana.' (Best: California.) Origin: Winters, CA. The large flattened fruit is a deep reddish-blue with light amber flesh. The vigorous tree is very productive. The fruit turns red when cooked. Pollinator: self. Ripens: late July. Available: (10), (32), (35).

'Ozark Premier.' (Best: South and Southwest.) Origin: Mountain Grove, MO. The extremely large red fruit has yellow flesh. The trees are hardy and productive. Pollinator: self. Ripens: about August 1. Available: wide distribution, especially in South.

Late

'Elephant Heart.' (Best: California, North.) Origin: Sebastopol, CA (Luther Burbank). The large, thick-skinned fruit is mottled purple and green. The flesh is blood red. Trees are strong and hardy. Fruit ripens over a long period. Pollinator: 'Santa Rosa.' Ripens: late July, August. Available: (10), (15), (32), (34), (45).

Hardy plums

These plums were especially selected and bred for the coldest northern and Great Plains climates.

'Pipestone.' Origin: Excelsior, MN. The large, red fruit has tough skin that is easy to peel. The flesh is yellow, of excellent quality but somewhat stringy. The tree is vigorous and hardy, of reliable performance in cold regions. Pollinator: 'Toka,' 'Superior.' Available: (12), (20), (22), (29), (44sD).

'Superior.' Origin: Excelsior, MN. Large, conical red fruit with russet dots and heavy bloom. The flesh is yellow and firm, excellent for eating fresh. The tree bears very young and prolifically. Pollinator: 'Toka.' Available: (12), (13D), (17D), (20D), (23), (26D), (27), (29).

'Toka.' Origin: Excelsior, MN. The large, pointed fruit is a medium red, often described as apricot-colored. The flesh is firm and yellow with a rich, spicy flavor. The tree is a heavy producer, spreading and medium-sized, but may be short-lived. Pollinator: 'Superior.' Available: (12), (20), (44).

'Underwood.' Origin: Excelsior, MN. The very large, red, freestone plum has golden yellow flesh. Somewhat stringy but of good dessert quality. Ripening extends over a long season from July. The tree is vigorous, among the most hardy. Pollinator: 'Superior.' Available: (12), (13), (17), (29), (34).

'Waneta.' Origin: South Dakota. Large, reddish-purple fruit with yellow flesh. Bears dependably every year. Pollinator: 'Superior.' Available: (10), (13), (17).

Apricots

In the colder regions of the country, the selection of apricot varieties is limited, since they bloom early and may suffer frost damage. In recent years, however, a number of hybrids with hardy Manchurian apricots have been produced to fill the gap, and now varieties such as 'Moongold' and 'Sungold' will fruit fairly regularly even in the northern plains. The choice of varieties widens in milder regions, and more tender varieties, such as 'Moorpark,' will bear in the eastern states.

The size of the tree

Even the dwarfed apricots on special rootstocks produce fair-sized trees, and a full-sized tree will fill a 25-foot-

Standard   Semidwarf   Genetic Dwarf

square site, but you can train the tree to branch high and use it in the landscape as a shade tree. See the silhouettes for comparison.

Where is the fruit?

Apricots, like plums, bear on spurs that produce for two to four years and then need to be pruned out and replaced with younger wood. See the sketch above right. Fruit may form in the second year, but don't expect a heavy crop until the third or fourth year. Trees are fairly long-lived and may last from 15 to 30 years, depending on location and care.

Pollination for apricots

Many apricots are self-fruitful, but in the colder regions it is usually best to plant a second variety for pollination to

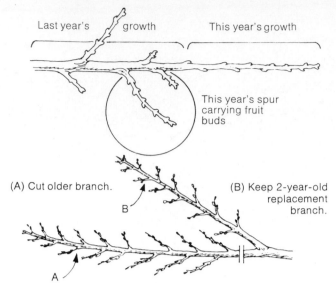

Last year's growth   This year's growth

This year's spur carrying fruit buds

(A) Cut older branch.   (B) Keep 2-year-old replacement branch.

encourage the heaviest fruit set possible. Frost damage may remove many of the young fruits.

Pruning and thinning for good crops

See pruning details on page 94. You need to head back long new whips by a half and remove the oldest fruiting wood. Generally, thinning is natural, either from frost or from natural drop in early summer. If your tree sets very heavily, you will get larger fruit by thinning to two inches between each piece.

Space-saver planting

Use two or three varieties in one hole to save space and provide a pollinizer and choice of fruit. Dwarf trees are best for this. Apricots can also be used as stock plants for grafts. Plums do well on apricot stock, and peaches may take, although the union is weak. Your apricot tree can bear several different fruits over a long season when you mix grafts.

Pests and disease

Brown rot and bacterial gumming are serious pests. See details for care on pages 74 to 77.

Apricots grow in landscape settings but require deep watering to thoroughly soak roots.

The variety list

Check for climate adaptation and pollinizing requirements, and be sure to buy hardy trees in the colder regions. The "D" after catalog numbers means dwarf trees are available.

'Alfred.' Origin: Geneva, NY. The fruit is small and round, of a bright orange color with juicy orange flesh. The tree is hardy and productive, flowering late enough to be a regular bearer in southern Michigan. The fruit ripens there in early August. Available: (28), (32).

'Curtis.' Origin: Charlotte, MI. A medium-sized golden fruit with a bright red blush. The flesh is firm and of excellent flavor when ripe. The tree is tall, open, slow-growing. Fruit ripens about the end of July in Michigan and is inclined to drop when ripe. Available: (32).

'Early Golden.' A medium-to-large, pale yellow fruit blushed red, with smooth skin and fine flavor. Ripens in mid-August in New York. Available: (2D), (4D), (8), (10), (13), (17D), (23D), (27).

'Goldcot.' Origin: South Haven, MI. The fruit is medium to large and nearly round with thick golden skin. The flesh is a medium-orange and firm. Good fresh or cooked, although it may darken when canned. The tree is strong with horizontal scaffolds. There is a tendency to overset and bear in alternate years unless thinned. Fruit ripens about July 20 in Michigan. Available: (2), (11), (14D), (20D), (22), (32).

'Golden Giant.' Patented by supplier. A very large golden orange fruit with a light blush, juicy, and of good flavor. The tree bears heavily. Successful in Iowa. Available: (20D).

'Hardy Iowa.' Origin: Glenwood, IA. A hardy chance seedling sold by the propagator. The fruit is pale yellow and rather small with thin skin. Flesh is very sweet. The tree is a prolific bearer and flowers late, escaping frost. For fresh fruit or pie and preserves. Available: (13).

'Henderson.' Origin: Geneva, NY. A large, round, yellow fruit with a light blush. The thick, yellow flesh is sweet and of good quality. The tree is vigorous with shiny foliage and a soft pink bloom. Available: (13).

'Hungarian.' The fruit is a rounded oval of solid golden color and particularly fine flavor. Very good for drying. It is less hardy than many other varieties listed here, may fail in late-spring zones. Available: (20D), (33D), (34).

'Manchu.' Origin: Brookings, SD (A Hansen introduction). This is a seedling of the native Manchurian apricot, and bears large yellow fruit that are excellent for cooking and can be eaten fresh. The tree is large and heavy-bearing. Available: (17).

'Moongold.' Origin: Excelsior, MN. A hybrid with 'Manchu' as one parent. The same cross produced 'Sungold' (below) and the two must be planted together for pollination. The fruit is orange with tough skin. The flesh is orange-yellow and of very good quality. The tree is a spreading, medium-sized plant. Fruit ripens in Minnesota in late July before Sungold. Available: (12), (14D), (17), (20), (26), (27), (31), (33).

'Moorpark.' Origin: Hertford, England (1760). The variety is considered by many to be the standard of excellence among apricots. The large fruit is orange with a deep blush, sometimes overlaid with dots of brown and red. The flesh is orange, of excellent flavor and with a pronounced and agreeable perfume. Ripening is uneven, with half the fruit still green when the first half ripens. This is unimportant in the home garden since the gardener can wait until the second half ripens to eat the fruit fresh. For canning, half the fruit is either too firm or too soft. The tree does well in all but the most extreme climates. Available: Wide distribution.

'Stella.' A hardy Russian apricot. The fruit is golden yellow and of good quality. The tree succeeds where a peach will grow. Available: (2), (14D).

'Sungold.' Origin: Excelsior, MN. A selection from the same cross as 'Moongold' and must be planted with 'Moongold' for pollination. The fruit is rounded and of medium size with a tender, golden skin blushed orange. Flavor is mild and sweet, and the fruit is good fresh or preserved. The tree is upright and vigorous, of medium size. The fruit ripens somewhat later than 'Moongold.' Available: (12), (17), (20), (26), (27D), (31).

Pick heavy crops firm and ripe and try drying them for winter.

Cherries

Sweet cherries, so good that gardeners have tried them in almost every climate of the world, are finicky in really cold regions where fall freezes damage them before they reach full dormancy. Even so, there are extensive commercial plantings near the Great Lakes. Sour cherries or pie cherries grow well over a much wider area and the dwarf 'Meteor' and 'Northstar' pie cherries were developed for Minnesota winters. In the Plains states, the best bet is a bush cherry such as the 'Hansen' or the sand cherry.

Where a sweet or pie cherry is a borderline crop, you may be successful anyway if you protect the tree. Don't feed the tree or force new growth after midsummer. In fall, mulch the root zone with six inches of organic mulch and hold it down with chicken wire. Plant behind a windbreak, and try protecting the main branches and trunk with a thick burlap wrap, removing it when weather warms.

The size of the tree

Cherries grow in many sizes as the silhouettes here show. Bush varieties reach six to eight feet tall and spread about as wide. The dwarf sour cherries, 'Meteor' and 'Northstar,' grow to about eight feet or a little more but have a single trunk. Standard-sized sour cherries and sweet cherries on dwarfing roots both reach 15 to 20 feet in height. A standard sweet cherry is the largest of the lot, and can equal a small oak in size if the climate doesn't do it in.

Where is the fruit?

All cherries bear on long-lived spurs. Those on tree cherries can produce for 10 years and more, and begin to

'Montmorency' is common pie cherry with scarlet skin.

bear along two-year-old branches. Count on the first crops in the third or fourth year after planting. Bush cherries may bear sooner.

Standard   Sour   Semi-dwarf   Bush   Genetic Dwarf

Pollination of cherries

Sweet cherries all need a pollinizer with the exception of the new variety 'Stella.' 'Windsor' is a good pollinizer and bears well itself, but always plant at least two varieties, or use a graft on a single tree. Sour cherries are self-fruitful, as are the bush cherries.

Pruning and thinning

Cherries need no thinning, and little pruning after the first two seasons of growth. See page 92 for methods of developing wide crotches and apply them to young sour cherries. Sweet cherries may need heading back in the first years of growth to encourage branching. See page 93.

Space-saver planting

The bush cherries and dwarf pie cherries make fine hedges and screens, with lovely bloom and a good crop. Larger cherries can be planted with two or more varieties in a single hole, or grafted for a choice of fruit and good pollination.

Pests and disease

Birds are a major pest, but cherries also need attention for fruit flies, slugs (actually an insect larva) and bacterial gumming. See details on pages 74 to 77.

The variety list

Check pollination carefully if you try a sweet cherry. For any cherry, check the recommended climate area. If you try a cherry outside its zone, offer as much protection as possible in fall and winter.

Early

'Black Tartarian.' This medium-sized black cherry is fairly firm when picked, but softens quickly. The trees are widely planted since this is one of the earliest cherries and an excellent pollinator for many others. Trees are erect and vigorous. Pollinator: any sweet cherry. Available: wide distribution.

'Sam.' Origin: Summerland, B.C. A medium to-large, black-fruited cherry that is firm and juicy, of good quality. The fruit resists cracking. The tree is very vigorous, and bears heavy crops. Pollinator: 'Bing,' 'Lambert,' 'Van.' Available: (1), (7), (35), (44sD).

Midseason

'Bing.' The standard for black sweet cherries. The fruit is very deep mahogany-red, firm and fleshy, and very juicy. The tree is spreading and produces heavy crops. 'Bing' is subject to cracking and doubling of fruit, and the tree suffers from bacterial attack in humid climates. Not easy to grow but a favorite of many. Pollinator: 'Black Republican,' 'Sam,' 'Van,' 'Black Tartarian.' (NOT 'Napoleon,' or 'Lambert.') Available: wide distribution.

'Emperor Francis.' A large yellow, blushed cherry resembling 'Napoleon,' but redder and more resistant to cracking. The tree is very productive and hardier than 'Napoleon.' Flesh is very firm. Pollinator: 'Hedelfingen,' 'Gold.' (NOT: 'Windsor,' 'Napoleon.') Available (1), (2), (4), (8), (23), (27), (28), (34), (44sD).

'Gold.' This is a yellow cherry that is very resistant to cracking. Tree and blossoms are especially hardy and very productive. It originated in Nebraska where it withstands −30 degrees. Original fruit small, but some strains larger. Pollinator: any sweet cherry. Available: (34), (44sD).

'Kansas Sweet' ('Hansen Sweet'). Origin: Wichita, KS. Not really a sweet cherry, but a fairly sweet form of the pie cherry group. The fruit is red with firm flesh, palatable fresh and good in pie. The tree and blossoms are hardy in Kansas. Pollinator: self-fruitful. Available: (6), (10), (13), (20D).

'Royal Ann' ('Napoleon'). Very old French variety. This is the standard for yellow, blushed cherries. It is the major brining cherry, appearing in commerce as candy and maraschino cherries. The firm, juicy fruit is excellent fresh and good for canning. The tree is very large and extremely productive, upright, but spreading widely with age. It is relatively tender, although the buds tolerate some cold. Pollinator: 'Corum,' 'Windsor,' 'Hedelfingen.' (NOT 'Bing' or 'Lambert.') Available: wide distribution.

'Schmidt.' A German variety. 'Schmidt' replaces 'Bing' as a major commercial black cherry in the East. The fruit is large and mahogany-colored with thick skin. The wine-red flesh is sweet but somewhat astringent. The large and vigorous tree is upright and spreading. It is hardy, but the fruit buds are fairly tender. Pollinator: 'Bing,' 'Lambert,' 'Napoleon.' Available: (2), (8), (14), (18), (23), (25), (27), (34), (44sD).

'Van.' Origin: Summerland, B.C. A large, dark fruit with some resistance to cracking, on a tree that is very hardy. 'Van' is especially good in borderline areas since it has a strong tendency to overset and therefore may produce a crop when other cherries fail. It bears from one to three years earlier than 'Bing.' Pollinator: 'Bing,' 'Lambert,' 'Napoleon,' any other. Available: wide distribution.

'Yellow Glass.' Especially hardy. The clear yellow fruit is the size of a pie cherry but sweet. Pollinator: 'Black Tartarian.' Available: (6), (17), (20), (26).

Late

'Hedelfingen.' A German variety. The variety bears dark, medium-sized fruit with meaty, firm flesh. One strain resists cracking, but some trees sold under this name are not crack resistant. The tree is only moderately hardy, of a spreading and drooping form, but bears heavily. Pollinator: any sweet cherry listed here. Available: (1), (2), (14), (23), (28), (34), (44sD).

'Lambert.' The fruit is large and dark, ripening later than 'Bing' but similar to it. The tree is more widely adapted than 'Bing' but it bears erratically in many eastern areas and is more difficult to train and prune. The strongly upright growth produces weak crotches if left untrained. Pollinator: 'Van,' 'Rainier.' (NOT 'Bing,' 'Napoleon,' 'Emperor Francis.') Available: wide distribution.

'Windsor.' The standard late, dark, commercial cherry in the East. The fruit is fairly small and not as firm as 'Bing' or 'Lambert.' However it is very bud-hardy and can be counted on for a crop. This is a fine choice for difficult borderline areas where other cherries may fail. The tree is medium-sized and vigorous with a good spread and it bears heavily. Pollinator: any sweet cherry, except 'Van' and 'Emperor Francis.' Available: wide distribution.

Sour cherries (pie cherries)

The following varieties are all self-fruitful. They will pollinate sweet cherries in mild climate areas. There are two types: the amarelle with clear juice and yellow flesh, and the morello with red juice and flesh. In the coldest northern climates the amarelle is the commercial cherry.

'Early Richmond.' An amarelle that is especially hardy. The fruit is small, round, and red, excellent for pie, jam, and preserves. It is astringent when eaten fresh. The tree is small, reaching 15 to 20 feet. Available: (2), (4), (14), (18), (20), (25), (26), (34), (36), (40).

'English Morello.' A morello. The fruit is medium-sized and dark red, resisting cracking. It has tart, firm flesh, good for cooking and canning. The tree is small and hardy, with drooping branches but only moderate vigor and productivity. Late-ripening. Available: (10), (28).

'Meteor.' An amarelle. Origin: Excelsior, MN. A genetic dwarf that reaches only about ten feet tall. The fruit is bright red and large for a pie cherry, with clear yellow flesh. The tree is especially hardy, but does well in milder climates too. An ideal home garden tree for all cherry climates. Available: wide distribution.

'Montmorency.' An amarelle. The standard sour cherry for commercial and home planting. The fruit is large and brilliant red with firm yellow flesh. It is strongly crack resistant. The tree is medium to large, vigorous and spreading. Various strains have slightly different ripening times and fruit characteristics. Available: wide distribution.

'Northstar.' A morello. Origin: Excelsior, MN. Developed with 'Meteor,' this is another genetic dwarf, excellent for the home garden. The fruit is red with red flesh and is resistant to cracking. The small, attractive tree is vigorous and hardy. It is resistant to brown rot. Fruit ripens early but will hang on the tree for up to two weeks. Available: wide distribution.

Bush cherries

Bush cherries are attractive, many-stemmed shrubs derived from two separate sources: an Asian plant, the Nanking cherry, and the native Western sand cherry. They are ornamental as well as fruit-producing, but require long periods of cold weather. The fruit, in heavy crops, is somewhat plumlike.

'Hansen Bush Cherry.' Origin: South Dakota. This is a selection from seedlings of the Nanking cherry. The fruit is dark to red depending on the selection, and the plant begins bearing in the first year after planting. The shrub is an excellent ornamental with heavy bloom, and reaches four to five feet tall with an even broader spread. Use the fruit fresh, in cooking, or in preserves. Available: (2), (8), (13), (14), (17), (23), (27), (29).

Western Sand Cherry. Many improved varieties are sold, with fruit ranging from black, to red, and yellow. All bear heavily and are attractive in flower.

'Black Beauty.' Black fruit. Available: (13), (17).
'Brooks.' Maroon fruit. Available: (13), (17).
'Golden Boy.' Yellow fruit. Available: (13).
'South Dakota.' Deep red fruit. Available: (13).

Genetic dwarf

A genetic dwarf variety of sweet cherry is available that is self-fruitful and ideal for containers. It may be used outside the sweet-cherry climate zone if you move it to cover in winter.

'Garden Bing.' A 'Bing'-like dark red fruit on a plant that remains only a few feet high in a container, but grows to perhaps 8 feet in the ground. It is self-fruitful. Available: (38)

Crabapples

Fine for jellies, or pickled whole fruit, crabapples are also the most decorative of fruit trees. Flowers range from red to pink-and-white. Leaf color may be red, bronze, variegated red-green, or green. Fruits are of many sizes from tiny cherrylike crabs to large, yellow, pink-cheeked kinds. The varieties sold for flowers have edible fruit, but large-fruited kinds are better if your aim is mainly a shelf full of glasses of jelly.

The size of the tree

Crabapples range from shrublike, 10-foot plants to spreading trees 25 feet tall. The large-fruited kinds are at the larger end of the range.

Where is the fruit?

Crabapples, like eating apples, fruit on long-lived spurs, generally producing clusters of several fruits on each. Since crops are heavy, you can cut back new wood without losing anything.

Pollination

Crabapples are self-fruitful, but you can graft in several kinds to extend harvest.

Pruning and thinning

Train the young trees to a vase with three or four scaffolds. After the second year you can leave them alone, or cut them back to maintain size. No thinning of the crop is necessary.

Small-space planting

Use small varieties if you're crowded. If you have no space but want a light crop for jelly, graft a branch to an existing apple tree.

Pests and disease

Crabapples are subject to the same diseases as apples, and scab is a major problem for some varieties. Choose resistant kinds.

The variety list

We include both large-fruiting kinds and kinds that are mainly ornamental, but offer a good crop. Use red or pink fruits if you want pink jelly.

'Barbara Ann.' The dark reddish-purple, half-inch fruit has reddish pulp. Fruit is borne annually. The tree opens a profusion of two-inch purple-pink, full double flowers. It grows to about 25 feet tall. Reasonably disease-resistant. Ornamental.

'Chestnut.' The very large, bronzy-red fruit is large enough to make a good dessert or lunch-box fruit, and can be jellied as well, producing deep pink jelly. The flavor is especially pleasing. The tree is very hardy and of medium size, reasonably disease-resistant. Fruiting. (12), (17).

'Dolgo.' The smallish, oblong red fruit is juicy; jells easily if picked before full ripeness, makes a ruby-red jelly. The extremely hardy tree came from Russia. It is vigorous and productive, ripens fruit in September. Fruiting. Widely available.

'Florence.' The large yellow fruit has an attractive red blush. Use it for pale pink jelly or for whole-fruit pickling. The tree is medium-large and somewhat tender, so it is best planted in zone 3 or warmer regions. It ranges from fairly to very productive. Fruiting. Widely available.

'Hyslop.' Another yellow, fair-sized fruit, blushed with red. Use it for whole relishes, or for pale pink jelly. The tree is fairly hardy, and quite ornamental with single pink bloom. Fruiting. (6), (14), (34), (44).

'Katherine.' The tiny fruits are yellow with a heavy red blush, very attractive on the tree, and can be made into a pink jelly. The tree is small, slow-growing, and fairly hardy, but it flowers and fruits every other year. It reaches about 15 feet tall and is reasonably disease-resistant. The two-inch flowers are fully double; open pale pink, then fade to white. Ornamental.

'Siberian Crab' is ornamental, makes good jellies.

'Barbara Ann' is a dark-fruited ornamental.

'Dolgo' is red-fruited with abundant blooms.

Large, single 'Dolgo' flower is a treat in spring.

'Montreal Beauty.' A medium-sized green fruit, striped red. This variety will serve for jelly or can be used as a jelling base for mint or rose geranium jellies. The medium-to-large tree is hardy and fairly disease-resistant. Fruiting. Locally available.

'Profusion.' Tiny scarlet fruits are good in jellies. The somewhat spreading tree is small (to about 15 feet) and produces small single flowers that are deep red in bud, then open to purplish-red to blue-pink. The tree is moderately susceptible to mildew. Ornamental.

'Siberian Crab.' The medium-sized fruit is a clear scarlet and very abundant. Use it for jelly or pickled whole fruits. The vase-shaped tree reaches 15 to as much as 30 feet, depending on climate and soil. The one-inch white flowers are fragrant. There are disease-resistant forms

of this tree, but others are subject to various diseases. Ornamental.

'Transcendent.' The large yellow fruits are blushed on one side with pink. Use them for clear jellies or eat them if you like the wild, astringent flavor. The medium-to-large tree is somewhat disease-resistant, but not very hardy. Plant in zone 3 or warmer. Fruiting. (7), (19), (35).

'Whitney.' An old favorite that has very large fruit, good for fresh eating, jelly, preserves, or apple butter. The color is yellow with red stripes. The tree is hardy, medium-to-large and reasonably disease-resistant. Fruiting. Widely available.

'Young America.' Fairly new variety with large and abundant red fruit that makes a clear red jelly with a splendid flavor. The tree is especially vigorous and hardy, and ripens fruit about mid-September. Fruiting. (28).

Tiny 'Katherine' is usable in jelly.

'Profusion' makes good jelly and is ornamental.

Home garden specialties

At home you can grow many fine fruits that never show up on a market shelf. Some are old favorites, some are ornamental, many are extra hardy, in sizes from big trees to tiny shrubs.

Some good fruit plants are overlooked by gardeners, just because nurseries don't always have them. And even well-known old favorites may be neglected as garden plants if tradition determines that you should gather them wild.

But plant breeders and nurserymen are catching up now on many plants that were always wild in Granny's day, and gardeners are recognizing the food value of many fruiting ornamentals.

American persimmon

The American persimmon is called, botanically, *Diospyros virginiana,* and it belongs to the same family of plants as the ebony tree of southern Asia. The tree grows as a native from Connecticut to Kansas and then southward, but it won't take the extreme cold of the Plains or northern New England.

Persimmon foliage is large and glossy, with leaves reaching up to six inches in length. The new spring leaves are bronze or reddish, and in fall they turn to shades of yellow, pink, and red. The two-inch fruit hangs on into the first frosts and is orange with a red blush. Eat it when it softens, or use it as you would applesauce or bananas in a spiced fruit bread or steamed pudding. If you want to store some, mash the soft pulp out of the skin for freezing, and discard the tough skin.

Use a persimmon tree as an attractive background plant in a shrub border, or in front of evergreens where it shows off its leaves and fruit best. It will also grow well as a single lawn tree, but you'll have a problem in late fall when the soft fruit drops and squashes.

The size of the tree
Persimmons grow as tall as 30 feet, but can be kept smaller by light pruning.

Small-space planting
You can try a persimmon as an informal espalier against a wall. The fruit is most attractive and easier to harvest.

Where does the fruit grow?
Fruit is borne on new wood. On a naturally shaped tree it will set on the outer portion.

◁

Elderberries for wine or jelly are larger and better if you grow them in your own garden.

Pruning and thinning
Prune the young tree for a strong scaffold, then leave it alone unless you are training it as a wall plant. Thinning is unnecessary, but with a lawn tree, you should pick all the fruit as the first ones begin to soften or you will find a mess as fully ripe fruit drops.

Pollination
American persimmons are dioecious, which means that some trees are male, producing pollen but no fruit, while others are female. You need a female tree for fruit with a male close by. Plant both unless you have wild trees near your garden. An occasional improved variety has fruit crops without pollination, but these are still experimental.

Elder blossoms are beautiful, and you can fry them in batter.

Quince, an old favorite, is fine garden fruit.

Pests and disease
You are unlikely to have much difficulty with a persimmon.

The variety list
You can buy persimmons of the native sort at the following nurseries: (5) (13) (15) (17) (36). You'll probably have to take your chances with the selection sold, but some good ones are 'Early Golden,' 'Garretson,' 'Hicks,' 'John Rick,' and 'Juhl.'

Buffalo-berry

The buffalo-berry, *Shepherdia argentea* is a native plant in the Great Plains, and is also called rabbit-berry and Nebraska currant. It grows wild from Minnesota to Saskatchewan, and south to Kansas. It is both extremely hardy and drought-tolerant.

Use buffalo-berry as a windbreak or shelter plant where its silvery leaves add interest and contrast to a row of evergreens. The bright berry clusters are highly ornamental in their season.

The size of the tree
This is a small tree or large shrub, growing to about 10 feet tall.

Where is the fruit?
Fruit clusters ripen all along the outer branches, but harvest is difficult because of the thorns, so be careful or wear gloves.

Other information
You don't need to prune the plants, especially if you want them to fill in as windbreak trees. The plants are heavily productive of small scarlet berries that ripen over a long period from July to fall and can be made into a good,

pretty jelly. Don't store the juice once you've extracted it, as it may transfer its odor to other foods in the refrigerator. It is high in vitamin C. Available: (12), (17), (32).

Cherry plum

Worthwhile in all the colder regions of the country both for ornament and fruit, the cherry plum blooms and fruits heavily, and many improved varieties are available. Don't confuse it with the European cherry plum (myrobalan). It's not the same thing. The cherry plums are derived by crossing American native plums with other related fruit, and they are generally very hardy. Among the parents of many cherry plums is the Western sand cherry, *Prunus besseyi,* which is also a good garden plant. We include another native in this list that is not strictly a cherry plum, and is somewhat less hardy. The beach plum *(Prunus maritima)* gives good crops of small fruit along the Atlantic Coast as far north as Maine.

The size of the plant
Cherry plums tend to be low, shrubby plants with many stems, spreading fairly wide and growing to four to eight feet tall, depending on the variety.

Small-space planting
All the cherry plums are excellent hedge and border plants, or you can grow them among ornamental shrubs. They need sun to set a good crop.

Where does the fruit grow?
The plants flower and fruit all along the branches and may begin to fruit the first year after planting.

Pruning
You can leave them alone, or train them in the early years to a trunk to make a little tree. They need constant attention

Fruits of the rose family often take this form.

Beach plum is delicious, and beautiful in flower.

in this form or they will revert to shrubs since they sucker readily.

Pollination

Most are self-fertile.

Pests and disease

The plants give little difficulty.

The variety list

Your nursery may have other varieties, but these are among the most widely available.

Beach plum. A native coastal plant along the Atlantic, the fruit is red-purple, good for jellies, plum butter. The plant grows to six to ten feet tall, spreading fairly wide and thrives on poor, sandy soil. Plant two or more for cross pollination and better crops. Available: (17), (23), (32).

'Compass.' An old variety that yields very heavy crops of red fruit in the second year after planting. The shrub reaches eight feet tall. You can eat the fruit fresh or make jams, jellies, or preserves. Available: (12), (17).

'Delight.' A purple fruit on a fairly small shrub. It ripens in midsummer and holds on for weeks without spoiling. Needs another plant as a pollinizer. Available: (38).

'Oka.' An old variety from the South Dakota Experiment Station. The one-inch fruit is deep purple-red with dark red flesh. It ripens from mid-August to early September and hangs on for up to three weeks after ripening. The plant may have a treelike shape, but stays small. Available: (13), (17).

'Opata.' An old variety with a purplish skin and green flesh. The plant is small, to about six feet. Available: (10).

'Sapa.' A very dark fruit, nearly black with flesh the same. The shrub may grow treelike. The fruit is of particularly fine, sweet flavor. Available: (10), (12), (17), (40).

'Sapalta.' A Canadian selection that resembles 'Sapa' but may be freestone. Available: (12).

Western sand cherry. A native of the Plains. The dark red-purple fruit grows on a five-foot shrub and is excellent for natural hedges. It produces the year after planting and can be eaten fresh or cooked. Available: (17), (32).

Cornelian-cherry

The cornelian-cherry, *Cornus mas,* is a dogwood, and is usually sold as an ornamental. It blooms very early (as early as February) on bare twigs, producing clustered yellow flowers. It will grow to about 15 feet tall, either as a shrub or a small tree, depending on your training. The shiny green leaves turn yellow or red in the fall. The bright scarlet fruits grow up to three-quarters of an inch long and ripen as the leaves turn, about September. They are usually very acid, making fine preserves or jelly. Available: (32).

Cranberry

The cranberry *(Vaccinium macrocarpon)* and the related lingonberry *(V. vitis-idaea)* are hard to find in nurseries although cranberries are grown in many regions commercially, and lingonberries can be found if you search them out. Either is worth the effort, not only for the fruit, but also for the plants that are low and spreading, attractive even as large-scale ground covers. They both like fairly acid and very light soils, but they do not need bog conditions even though commercial cranberries are usually grown in flooded bogs.

Use cranberries in the familiar sauces and relishes, and use lingonberries with some sugar to make beautiful, bright red and slightly astringent fruit sauce to serve as you do cranberry sauce, or in the Swedish manner with pancakes.

Both fruit and foliage of the cranberry are decorative.

Cranberry ground cover offers an edible crop.

Elderberry

Blue (or black) elderberries grow wild over much of the United States and Canada. The several kinds all belong to the genus *Sambucus.* (Red-fruited kinds are poisonous.) Since even wild bushes fruit heavily in most years, people have been gathering elder fruit for wine, pie, and jelly for many, many years. Even the flower is edible if you dip it in fritter batter and fry it quickly to serve with syrup. It turns out like crisp lace and may even be good for you, since in Europe the flower is considered to have medicinal properties.

The plants themselves are familiar to most people. They are tall shrubs with many stems rising up and outward in a fountain. Occasionally a very old specimen turns into a gnarled small tree, but since elder wood is pithy and soft at the center, the tree shape is not very sturdy.

To use the fruit, wait until it is dark in color (the surface is covered with a dusty bloom). Then get help to strip the many stems if you want it for pie. For jelly or wine, just cut the heaviest part of the stem then crush the fruit, or heat it and pass it through the jelly bag. If you eat it before cooking you will find it laxative and perhaps bitter, but that changes with heat.

The size of the shrub

Elder bushes can reach about 20 feet and spread rather wide, but you can cut back the oldest stems from time to time to control size.

Pruning

Remove stems that have borne for several years to make way for younger growth. You'll need a small saw or big loppers.

Pollination

Plant two. The plants are almost entirely self-unfruitful.

Varieties

Some nurseries sell their own selections without a variety name. The following list elderberry in their catalog: (8), (12), (17). Here are some of the named varieties.

'Adams.' Origin: New York. There are a couple of these, with clusters and berries larger than the wild fruit and a bit easier to deal with in the kitchen. Ripens early August. They are selections from *S. canadensis.* Available: (6), (14), (23), (27).

'Johns.' A more vigorous plant than 'Adams' but not so productive. It ripens a few weeks later. Available: (6), (13), (14), (27).

'Kent.' From Nova Scotia. It resembles 'Adams' but ripens about ten days earlier. Available: (13).

'Nova.' Also from Nova Scotia. The large fruit ripens uniformly in the cluster, which is helpful. It is also sweeter than many varieties and fairly early ripening. The plants sucker easily. Available: (28).

'York.' From New York. This is the largest berry of all, in heavy clusters. The plant is very large and productive. It ripens late, after 'Adams.' Available: (28).

Highbush cranberry

Not a cranberry at all, this beautiful ornamental shrub is a viburnum. The American form is *V. trilobum,* and the European form, very similar, is *V. opulus.* You must buy the American plant for eating, since the European

Harvest the red fruit of the highbush cranberry (Viburnum) while still firm to use for jellies.

may taste bitter, but both are sold as cranberrybush, so ask or taste if possible.

This is a close relative of the elderberry and grows to about the same size with a similar clumping habit.

The flowers of the high-bush cranberry are exquisite clusters that resemble the lacecap hydrangea, with small entire flowers in the center and large sterile ones at the edges. They are followed by clusters of scarlet fruit. For jellies, harvest the fruit while it is quite firm but well colored. Overripe fruit has a disagreeable odor when heated, although this will disappear when it is jellied and cooled again. The odor of the juice can transfer to other foods if it is stored in the refrigerator, so don't hold it after extraction.

There are a number of named selections, but our sources offer the species plant rather than named plants. Available: (12), (13), (32).

Mahonia

This prickly-leafed ornamental is usually called Oregon-grape, since the earlier pioneers on the Oregon trail used it for jellies. The attractive plant comes in many forms, from very tall multiple-stalked shrubs to low forms, useful as ground cover. It has yellow clusters of flowers above the foliage followed by dark blue berries with a bloom. It is closely related to the barberries, which are also good jelly plants as well as fine hedge or border shrubs. Available: (23), (33), (39).

Medlar

The medlar may be difficult to find, but it's available if you inquire. It is handled by the Southmeadow Fruit Gardens,

(32) on our catalog list, but you may also find it locally. The botanical name is *Mespilus germanica*.

In Europe it is fairly popular, but in this country is hardly known. The fruit is rather like a large brown rose hip (it is in the rose family) and grows on a shrub or tree that is variable in height, but can reach 20 feet. Our only source offers 'Nottingham,' a small plant, and suggests planting it with the graft union below the soil surface to encourage scion rooting and greater vigor.

When the fruit ripens on the tree it is not yet edible. You must pick it and leave it in storage until it becomes over-ripe (or *'blet'* as the French say). It is then quite good fresh, or it may be made into a preserve or jelly. The medlar is close enough to the pear, botanically, that medlar grafts will take on a pear tree, and they will also take on quince or hawthorn, so you might try a branch of medlar on one of your other trees for a light crop of conversation-piece fruit.

The leaves of the medlar tree are downy, a bit like quince, and the flowers are large and white, fading to pink with age and very decorative. It blooms on the tips of current growth. The plant is not particular as to soil. Again drawing from our source catalog, we suggest a recipe they find good. Once medlars are well 'bletted,' extract the pulp with a food mill and fold it into sweetened whipped cream. Chill well and serve as a dessert mousse.

Mountain ash (Sorbus)

This small tree with its clusters of white bloom and heavy bunches of red berries is one of the most decorative ornamentals sold, but the berries are also good to eat, either fresh or in jellies. To eat berries fresh, hold them until "bletted" like a medlar. The tree is also known as the

Mountain ash is ornamental and berries are good to eat.

rowan. It grows rapidly to 20 or 30 feet tall and spreads to about 20 feet, although in the cooler regions it will probably be smaller. It is subject to fire blight, together with so many other members of the rose family, but is worth a try anyway. Available: wide distribution.

Pawpaw (Asimina triloba)

This Midwestern specialty is also called the winter banana, since its custardy flesh reminds many people of bananas. It is actually the only hardy member of a large tropical family of plants, the *Annonaceae,* which also contains the soursop and cherimoya.

The pawpaw tree varies a good bit in the wild, and can produce a shrubby thicket with its suckers, or grow treelike to 25 feet tall. Our sources do not list any of the improved variety names, although there is much experimentation with the fruit.

The fruit itself is long and rather narrow, reaching three to five inches, and is yellow when ripe. It then softens inside to a custardy consistency around several large brown seeds.

If you plant a pawpaw, be patient. It is slow to grow and slow to bear, although some of the improved kinds bear more quickly than wildings. It must have cross-pollination, which is no problem if you live where the trees grow wild. In the garden, if a tree fails to set fruit even though it produces its purple, fragrant bloom, try taking ripe pollen with a pencil eraser in the afternoon when it is ripe and loose, then touching it to the flower pistils in the morning when they are wet-looking. Available: (5), (13), (14), (17).

Pyracantha (firethorn)

A well known ornamental, the hardy species is *P. coccinea* with orange berries. You'll find it in many forms, from tall shrubs to low dwarfs. All bear quantities of white flowers followed by dense orange fruit the size of peas. Use them before they are dead ripe for a beautiful jelly. The somewhat similar cotoneaster also produces berries that will serve for jelly-making.

Quince (Cydonia oblonga)

This old favorite is no longer widely planted, but it should be. The naturally small trees produce lovely pink and white flowers at the branch tips, followed by large round or pear-shaped fruit covered with down, and with a delightful aroma. The fruit is very firm and fibrous, not good fresh unless you like (as some people do) a very tart, chewy fruit. Nothing is better, however for jelly or fruit candy, and quinces can also be used with apples for pie or sauce.

When you prepare juice for jelly, don't peel or core the fruit. Much of the pectin is in the skin and seeds. Cut it up, use a small amount of water to start the juice, and once it is cooked enough to soften, pass it through the jelly bag. Pass the pulp through a food mill to remove the skin and seeds and cook it with sugar until thickened. Then dry it on trays, dust it with powdered sugar and cut into pieces for delightful candy.

The size of the tree
Quince grows to about 12 to 15 feet. It will try to form a shrub, and you should discourage twigs along the trunk and suckers, as it will fruit better as a tree.

Mahonia's blue berries make a good jelly.

Orange pyracantha is another ornamental jelly plant.

Where is the fruit?

Fruit forms on branch tips of current growth, so winter pruning won't remove it, but don't cut back too much as the tree is subject to fire blight and the less soft growth the better.

Pollination

Quince is self-fertile.

Pests and disease

Fire blight is the worst problem, but the trees bear young, so if you lose one, and fire blight is not too severe in your area, try again. Spray for codling moth. Galls on branches are normal, so don't remove them.

The variety list

Many forms are available. The classic quince is pear-shaped, but the round kinds are just as good. NOTE: The Oriental or flowering quince is a different plant, *Chaenomeles.* It also has edible fruit, shaped like quince, but the plant is always a large shrub and the flowers are showy and dense along the branches, in shades of bright reddish-pink, salmon, and white.

'Champion.' A large pear-shaped variety with a tinge of green in the yellow skin and yellow flesh. It ripens in October. Available: (17).

'Orange.' (Also called 'Apple.') This is an old favorite with round, golden fruit and tender, orange-yellow flesh. Available: (23), (25), (34).

'Pineapple.' A round fruit with light golden skin and white flesh. The aroma is similar to pineapple. Available: (10), (15), (17), (45), (46).

'Smyrna.' The fruit is rounded to oblong with bright yellow skin and a strong fragrance. Available: (10), (15), (32), (45), (46).

'Van Deman.' A Luther Burbank creation with large fruit that ripens early and retains its flavor well when cooked. Available: (34).

Service-berry (Amelanchier)

This odd botanical name refers to a familiar plant, but as is so often the case, the same plant has a good many common names. It is called juneberry, service-berry, shadblow, and saskatoon among other things, and is a member of the rose family.

It is hardy, growing native in the Canadian Plains, and is an attractive ornamental, flowering early and fruiting the year after planting. It grows 10 to 15 feet tall, either as a shrub or a small tree. The best fruiting species is probably *A. alnifolia,* the saskatoon, but any species has edible fruit.

The fruit itself somewhat resembles tiny, blue-purple crabapples. (The color varies from cream to red to almost black, but the purple form is common.) It is small, to about a half inch across, and when fully ripe has the flavor of blueberries. It was once dried by the Indians, and it can be eaten fresh, cooked in pie, or canned. It is rich in vitamin C.

For landscape use it is ideal, since the white flowers are showy in spring, and the foliage colors well in fall. Any excess fruit will attract birds to the garden. Available: (12), (13), (14), (22), (23), (32), (33), (36).

A picture gallery

These are the sights of a fruit garden from the flowers of spring to the ripened fruits of summer and fall.

The contentment a gardener feels comes mainly from fleeting impressions, quickly gone, again repeated in other forms. It may be a morning when the sky clears revealing an orchard in full bloom, or the few seconds when a cluster of just-ripe cherries stands out from the leaves.

These are private moments. When you try to share them, searching out someone else to say, "Look—" the moment is past, the light has changed. So much of the beauty comes from your own feelings when, after months of dutiful care, your plants reward you.

The small fruits

A little sunlight and a pot is all you need to grow luscious breakfast strawberries, and many of the other small fruits offer rich rewards for a small investment of time and space.

The small-fruited plants return bumper crops with only a minimum of effort on your part, and several of the shrubby or vining plants also add beauty to the ornamental landscape.

In considering small fruits, space and the number of plants needed for a reasonable supply of fruit are factors to be worked out. If the plants are right for your climate and are given excellent care, the number of plants for a family of five would go something like this:

Strawberries: 25 (20 to 30 quarts)

Raspberries: 24 (20 to 30 quarts)

Blackberries: 12 (9 to 15 quarts)

Blueberries: 6 (9 to 15 quarts)

Currants: 2 (6 to 12 quarts)

Gooseberries: 2 (6 to 12 quarts)

Strawberries are without question the easiest to work into any space you may have available. Even on a south-facing apartment terrace you can produce a crop in containers such as strawberry jars or a moss-lined wire strawberry tree. An ideal plant for containers where you can find it is the European wild strawberry or *fraise des bois*. This plant won't make runners. It grows in a clump, so a container planting stays put instead of trying to invade the living room. You'll have to do some detective work to find a source for the plants.

The cane berries, raspberries and blackberries, take more space, although you can grow a few in large containers. Train them carefully along a fence or trellis and keep them pruned, and they won't take very much space, but they *will* produce heavy crops of fruit that you just can't buy, since the finest flavor disappears when farmers and greengrocers transport and hold the berries.

Blueberries, currants, and gooseberries make extremely ornamental shrubs, filled with bloom in spring and with decorative fruit in later seasons. Blueberries require light, acid soil and constant moisture, so try them where you would grow azaleas. Currants and gooseberries are an interim host to a serious disease of five-needle pines, so in some areas you're not allowed to plant them. Where they

◁

Top left: Large-fruited trailing blackberries.
Top right: Strawberries grow anywhere if you pick the right kind.
Bottom: Neat wooden frame holds trailing blackberries.

are permitted, nothing takes less care, is more decorative, or gives a more useful crop.

Grapes, of course, are among the best landscaping plants with their lush foliage, fall color, and interesting vines. Use them on arbors, against walls, as fences, or freestanding shrubs. Do choose varieties recommended for your climate, since grapes are touchy about the amount of heat they get.

Strawberries

If you have grown strawberries for any length of time, you know that flavor and yield are not exactly predictable. They vary from year to year depending upon spring growing conditions. Also, if you have gardened in several locations, you learn that what is the best variety in one place may only be fair in another. A good nurseryman is a big help, since he'll keep abreast of developments in plant breeding and offer plants that should succeed. Your County Agricultural Agent can help too, especially if you've had trouble in other seasons.

Strawberries are ideal container fruit.

Planting and care

Strawberries can be grown in either the matted-row or the hill system.

There are two types of matted rows. In one, all runners are allowed to grow; in the other, only the earliest to form remain, spaced about eight inches apart. The latter, spaced-runner system gives you larger berries, easier picking, and larger total yield. See the illustration for the arrangement of runners. The rows should be spaced three to four feet apart when you plant.

In the hill system, plants are 12 inches apart in the row and all runners are picked off. The rows are spaced about 12 to 15 inches apart in groups of three. Each group is separated by an aisle 24 to 30 inches wide so that you can walk among the plants to pick or care for them. The system lends itself to everbearing strawberries, or single-crop kinds that don't send out many runners.

To encourage vigorous growth of regular varieties, remove blossoms that appear the year the plants are set. The year that everbearing kinds are set, remove all blossoms until the middle of July. The later blossoms will produce a late summer and fall crop.

Plant strawberries in soil with good drainage, mound the planting site if you're not sure. See the illustration for proper planting depth. The new leaf bud in the center of each plant should sit exactly level with the soil surface.

Gardeners who grow strawberries in containers in a disease-free soil mix don't have to worry about verticillium wilt and red stele (root rot). Both are caused by soilborne fungus. When growing strawberries in containers or in garden soil, ask for plants that are certified as disease-free.

Mulching in winter

Winter protection is needed where alternate freezing and thawing of the soil may cause the plants to heave and break the roots. Low temperatures also injure the crowns of the plants. Straw is one of the best mulch materials.

Place straw three or four inches deep over the plants before the soil is frozen hard. Remove most of the mulch in spring when the center of a few plants shows a yellow-green color. You can leave an inch of loose straw, even add some fresh straw between rows. The plants will come up through it and it will help retain moisture in the soil and keep mud off the berries.

The variety list

Here are a few good plants for northern climates.

'Ardmore.' Late midseason. Missouri introduction. Large berries of good flavor. Color is yellowish-red outside,

Some modern hybrid strawberries are amazingy big. Their size is impressive but the flavor of smaller berries is often better.

lighter inside. Productive in heavy silt loam. Available: (4), (14), (31).

'Catskill.' Midseason. Large berries of good dessert quality and excellent for freezing. Fruit is not firm enough for distance shipping, but is a productive home garden variety. It is grown over a wide range of soil types from New England and New Jersey to southern Minnesota. Available: wide distribution.

'Cyclone.' Early. Iowa. Large berries of very good flavor and good for freezing. Plant is winter-hardy and resistant to foliage diseases. Well adapted in North Central States. Available: wide distribution.

'Dunlap.' Early to midseason. Illinois introduction, 1890. Medium-sized. Skin is dark crimson and flesh is deep red. Fruit is too soft to ship well but it's a good quality home-garden fruit. Plants are hardy and adapted to a wide range of soil types in northern Illinois, Iowa, Wisconsin, Minnesota, North Dakota, South Dakota, and Nebraska. Available: (12), (13), (14), (17), (20).

'Earlidawn.' Early. A fresh market and freezing variety. Berries are large and of good dessert quality. Moderately resistant to leaf spot and leaf scorch. Adapted to Maryland, north to New England. Available: (2), (4), (6), (14).

'Fairfax.' Medium-early. Maryland, 1923. Attractive medium-sized berries, bright red outside, deep red inside.

Plastic mulch helps retain water, warm soil.

Plant pockets among bricks is interesting method.

Excellent flavor. Plants are especially productive when late-season runners are picked off. 'Fairfax' is grown from southern New England to Maryland. Available: (2), (4), (14), (16), (31).

'Fletcher.' Midseason. New York. Berries are medium in size with a medium-red, glossy, tender skin. Excellent flavor quality. Very good for freezing. Well adapted to New York and New England. Available: (14), (31).

'Howard 17' ('Premier'). Early. Massachusetts. Medium-sized berries of good quality. Productive. Resistant to leaf diseases and highly tolerant of virus disease. Locally available.

'Jerseybelle.' Late. New Jersey, 1955. Noted for its large showy fruits. Has a mild flavor but is not adapted to freezing. Very susceptible to diseases. Available: (2), (4), (6), (8), (14).

'Midland.' Very early. Maryland, 1929. Large glossy berries with deep red flesh. Very good to excellent for fresh use. Freezes well. Best when grown in the hill system. Adapted from southern New England to Virginia, and west to Iowa and Kansas. Available: (2), (14).

'Midway.' Midseason. Maryland, 1951. Large berries of good to very good dessert quality. Good for freezing. Susceptible to leaf spot, leaf scorch, and verticillium wilt. Widely planted in Michigan. Available: wide distribution.

'Pocahontas.' Early. Maryland, 1946. Good for use fresh, frozen, in preserves. Plants vigorous, resistant to leaf scorch. Adapted from southern New England south to Norfolk. Available: (2), (4), (6), (20).

'Raritan.' Midseason. New Jersey, 1968. Medium-sized plants but very productive. Large firm berries of good flavor. Available: (2), (4), (6), (14), (31).

'Redstar.' Late. Maryland, 1951. Large berries of good to very good dessert quality. Plants are tolerant of virus diseases, leaf spot, and leaf scorch. Grown from southern New England south to Maryland and west to Missouri and Iowa. Available: (2), (4), (14).

'Sparkle.' Midseason. Productive plants. Bright red, attractive berry, fairly soft, good flavor. Berry size is good in early picking, but small in later ones. Available: wide distribution.

'Surecrop.' Early. Maryland. Large, round, glossy, firm, and of good dessert quality. Large plants should be spaced six to nine inches apart for top production. Resistant to red stele, verticillium wilt, leaf spot, leaf scorch, and drought. Available: wide distribution.

'Trumpeter.' Late. Minnesota, 1960. Medium-sized berries, soft and glossy and of very good flavor. Winter-hardy and

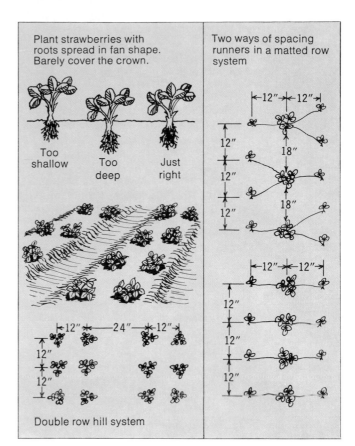

Plant strawberries with roots spread in fan shape. Barely cover the crown.

Too shallow — Too deep — Just right

Two ways of spacing runners in a matted row system

Double row hill system

productive home-garden variety for the upper Mississippi Valley and Plains States. Available: (17).

Everbearing varieties

'Gem' ('Superfection' and 'Brilliant' are considered to be nearly identical to 'Gem'). Small, glossy, red, tart fruit of good dessert quality. Available: wide distribution.

'Geneva.' Plants large and vigorous, fruits well in June and throughout the summer and early autumn. Berries soft and highly flavored. Available: (4), (6), (13), (14).

'Ogallala.' Berries are dark red, soft, and of medium size. Good flavor and good for freezing. Vigorous grower and hardy. Available: wide distribution.

'Ozark Beauty.' Berries are large, sweet, and of good flavor. Bright red outside and inside. Production on mother plants, but not on runner plants during summer and fall. Available: wide distribution.

Permanent bird protection saves your crop the easy way.

Screen plants before the fruit ripens.

Raspberries

Raspberries are the hardiest of the cane berries, and perhaps the most worthwhile home garden crop for several reasons. First, prices for the market fruit are high, since care and labor are expensive. Then too, market raspberries are held and handled long enough that fruit loses its finest flavor and may be bruised. Home-garden fruit can be picked and eaten at its peak.

The thing that makes a raspberry a raspberry is the fact that it pulls free of its core when you pick it. Other bramble fruits take the core with them when you harvest. Real raspberries, though, come in a variety of colors, and a number of plant forms. The red raspberry is the most popular, but there are yellow, purple, and black fruits as well, and plants are trailing among red raspberries (and yellows), but stiff among purple and black forms.

Planting raspberries

Cut nursery plants to 6- to 12-inch stubs and plant them about two to four feet apart, and two inches deeper than they grew in the nursery row. Rows should be six or seven feet apart.

Where is the fruit?

On most raspberries fruit forms on side shoots along canes that grew the previous year. One group of red raspberries produces a little fruit at the top of current-season canes in fall, then a second crop on the rest of the cane the following year.

Pruning raspberries

See page 97 for instructions on pruning. New canes should be laid carefully along rows until time to prune away old canes, then lifted and trained. Pull out suckers between rows of red raspberries.

Pests and diseases

The real plague of red raspberries is verticillium wilt. If you know your soil is infected, it's not worth trying

When you pick a raspberry the core stays on the plant.

the fruit .Other diseases and pests can be controlled with sprays or resistant plants. Black raspberries succumb to viruses and should be planted at least 700 feet from any reds.

Winter protection of the plants

Raspberries are extremely hardy, so no special protection is needed except in the coldest mountain and plains climates. Where winter temperatures stay extremely low for long periods, and winds add to the chill, you should protect your plants.

Lay canes of the current season along the row or trellis, pinning portions that arch upward. Be careful not to snap them. Where mice are unlikely to be a problem, cover the canes with straw or sawdust to a depth of several inches, then cover the mulch with poultry netting to hold it in place. If you know that mouse damage is probable in winter, bury the canes in earth about two inches deep.

In spring, uncover the canes before they begin to leaf out, just as the buds swell. If the buds break while still covered, they will be extremely tender to even light frost.

Blackcaps produce abundantly on erect plants.

Ripe blackcap raspberries ready to pick.

Propagating raspberries

If you want to enlarge a planting, it's important to know the difference between black and red raspberries. Blacks and purples arch their canes to the ground and root at the tip to form new plants. If you want more, leave a few canes unpruned and in late summer pin them to the ground at the tip. Red raspberries send up root suckers. You can dig and replant them just before spring growth begins. Take a piece of root with them.

The variety list

Single-crop and everbearing raspberries may be red or yellow. They require training.

Single-crop

'Amber.' Yellow. Excellent dessert fruit. Available: (2).

'Hilton.' Late red. Largest of all reds. Very attractive and of excellent quality. Vigorous, productive, and hardy. Available: (2).

'Latham.' Old mid-to-late red. One of the hardiest, most vigorous and most reliable croppers. Fair quality. Available: wide distribution.

'Newburgh' (Often spelled 'Newberg'). Midseason red. Large, firm berries. Productive. Available: (3), (13), (17).

'Taylor.' Mid-to-late red. Attractive, firm berries of excellent quality. Vigorous and hardy. Locally available.

Everbearing (fall-bearing)

'Durham.' Summer and fall red. Extra good flavor. Very hardy. Available: (4), (14).

'Fallgold.' Golden yellow berries. Available: wide distribution.

'Fallred.' Large red berries ideal for canning, freezing. Available: wide distribution.

'Heritage.' Firm red berry, July and September. Available: (2), (3), (14), (20).

'Indian Summer.' Large red fruit of good quality and yield. Fall crop late, may freeze. Available: wide distribution.

'September.' Medium-to-large red berries. Vigorous and hardy. One of the best. Available: (5), (6), (17), (20).

Purple

Plants are tall and stiff.

'Amethyst.' Early. Good quality introduction from Iowa. Available: (8), (13), (20).

'Clyde.' Early. Large, firm, dark purple berry of excellent quality. Vigorous. Replacing 'Sodus,' 'Marion.' Available: (14), (27).

'Sodus.' Midseason. Large firm fruit of good quality, but tart. Productive. Available: (12), (13), (14), (17), (20).

Black (blackcap)

'Allen.' Large, attractive berry. Vigorous and productive plant. Available: (2), (14), (22), (23), (27).

'Black Hawk.' Late. Large berry, good flavor and yield. Available: wide distribution.

'Bristol.' Midseason. Good size and flavor. Good for canning, freezing. Available: (2), (6), (14), (20), (23), (27).

'Cumberland.' Old-timer. Produces large firm berries of good quality. Available: wide distribution.

'Logan' ('New Logan'). Medium-to-large, firm berries. Vigorous. Available: (2), (8), (14).

Use a double-wire trellis for the woven method of training.

Make the crossbar sturdy to hold weight.

The lowest wires help protect growing canes.

Use your trellis to protect crop from birds.

Blackberries

Blackberries come in two fairly distinct forms and have a number of different names, so it may seem that there are more kinds of fruit involved than is really the case.

Here are descriptions of the various kinds. (None is as hardy as a raspberry, which is an extremely close cousin.) The *blackberry* of ordinary conversation is a stiff-caned, fairly hardy plant that can stand by itself if properly pruned. The *dewberry* is tender, has limp, trailing canes, and is mainly grown in zone 5 and farther south. In addition, nurseries sell trailing plants from the Pacific Coast under their variety names, mainly 'Boysen' and 'Logan.' These will freeze without winter protection.

Choosing a variety

We divide our list into erect and trailing berries. The trailing berries are really too tender for culture without special protection, but the fruit tends to be more flavorful than the erect kinds. Erect blackberries are not recommended for zones 1 and 2, but will grow elsewhere, and may succeed in the North if you bundle up the canes in straw and burlap for the winter. You'll find the chore less painful if you wear gloves.

Planting blackberries

Cut the nursery plants to six-inch stubs and plant them at the same depth as they grew in the nursery row. Set them about four feet apart in rows six to nine feet apart. The stiff kinds need no trellis. Trailing kinds must have support as suggested here and on page 97.

Plant in early spring, a month before the last frost in northern areas. As soon as new growth begins, cut any stubs from the previous growing season to avoid anthracnose. You should burn these cuttings.

'Logan' is popular trailing berry everywhere.

Mild climate trailing berries, best in California or Gulf Coast, need winter protection when snow falls.

Mulches help keep soil moist, prevent weed growth, help to prevent suckers. Use several inches of any organic mulch. Some, such as fresh straw or sawdust, will require the addition of nitrogen. Use any high-nitrogen fertilizer at the rate of one-half pound to a pound per 100 square feet.

Don't fertilize too heavily or you will get lush plant growth at the expense of the crop.

Where is the fruit?

Blackberries fruit on twiggy side branches growing on canes of the previous season. The canes fruit only once and must be removed every year.

Pruning and training

See page 97 for pruning and training methods. The stiff-caned berries need no support, but you can confine them between two wires to cut back on space. Dewberries should be cut to the ground after fruiting and burned. The new growth of the last part of summer will fruit the following year and you'll save some trouble with disease. Keep suckers pulled between rows.

A note: If you bother or cut roots of blackberries, they will sucker badly. If you want more plants, chop off pieces of root beside the parent plants and set them in the new planting site like seed. If you don't want more plants, mulch the planting instead of cultivating for weed control.

Pests and disease

Blackberries are subject to enormous numbers of pests and diseases. You can save yourself a lot of trouble by buying certified plants and keeping them away from any wild plants. Some varieties resist some diseases. Spray for blackberry mite, and don't worry too much about all the rest.

The variety list

We begin with the more hardy erect varieties. Don't bother with the others unless you want the work of burying canes in winter as suggested under Raspberries on page 62. (They *do* taste pretty good and you might not mind the work.)

Hardy, erect berries

'Alfred.' A Michigan introduction that produces large firm berries early. Locally available.

'Bailey.' Originated in Geneva, NY. The fruit is large and medium firm, of good quality. The bush is reliably productive. Available: (13), (20).

'Darrow.' From Geneva, NY, 1958. The large fruit is irregular and black, with firm flesh of good quality. Ripens over a long period, perhaps into fall. The plant is vigorous and very hardy, a heavy producer. Available: wide distribution.

'Eldorado.' An old favorite that is entirely immune to orange rust. However, strains resembling 'Eldorado' are susceptible, so buy from a trustworthy source. Available: (14).

'Ebony King.' A purplish fruit from Michigan. The skin is black and glossy with a sweet, tangy flesh. It ripens early. The plant is upright and hardy, resists orange rust. Available: wide distribution.

'Hedrick.' From New York, 1950. The fruit is large, medium-firm, and tart. The bush is reliably productive. Locally available.

'Raven.' Early. From Maryland, 1962. The large fruit is of high quality, fresh or processed. The plant is erect, vigorous, and productive. Rather tender. Zone 5 only. Available: (2), (14).

'Smoothstem.' Late. From Maryland, 1965. The berries are large and black, on the soft side. The erect canes are thornless and perhaps more productive than 'Thornfree.' Available: (2), (13), (14).

'Thornfree.' Late. From Maryland, 1966. The medium-large fruit is tart and good. The semiupright canes reach eight feet unpinched, with up to 30 berries on each fruiting twig. Rather tender. Zone 5 only. Available: wide distribution.

Trailing berries
All are tender and need protection from cold as described in the raspberry section on page 62.

Blackberry shape ranges from round to cylindrical.

'Lucretia.' An early dewberry from North Carolina. It is probably the hardiest dewberry with large, long, soft berries. Zone 5 and winter protection. Available: (5), (13), (14), (17).

'Thornless Boysen.' A summer-bearing Pacific Coast berry. It is flavorful with a fine aroma, and grows on tender plants that must be trained as shown below or on page 97. Bury the canes for the winter. Zone 5 only. Available: wide distribution.

'Thornless Logan.' Another Pacific Coast berry. It is acid, good for jam and pie, or syrup for drink base. Bury the canes in winter. Zone 5 only. Available: (14), (17).

Trailing berries need support such as this woven trellis.

Blueberries

Blueberries demand just the right climate and planting soil, but take very little care if you provide the conditions they like. They are about as hardy as a peach, but need a fair amount of winter chill, and will not grow well in mild-winter climates.

Blueberries belong to the heath family, and count azaleas, rhododendrons, mountain-laurel *(Kalmia),* and huckleberries among their cousins. If any of these grow naturally near your garden, or if you have prepared an artificial site that suits them, then blueberries will do well too.

Blueberries like soil rich in organic material such as peat, and very acid, but extremely well drained. Soils such as these are usual in areas of high rainfall, which is lucky, since the berries need constant moisture, even though they will not tolerate standing water.

You'll find major commercial plantings of blueberries in New Jersey, especially Burlington and Atlantic Counties; in Michigan in favored areas of the lower peninsula; in Washington and Oregon; and to a certain extent in New York, Massachusetts, and Indiana.

Planting blueberries

The soil must be both acid and well drained. You will have to plant in raised beds if there is any chance of water standing around the roots for even a day. For both drainage and acidification, add large amounts of peat moss or other organic material to the planting soil; up to three-quarters peat moss by volume for soils that tend to be heavy. Never add manure; it is alkaline.

Dig the planting hole somewhat broader and deeper than the roots of the young plant. Never cramp the roots into a small hole. Spread them in a wide hole and press soil firmly over them.

Set high-bush blueberry plants about four feet apart, and at the same level as in the nursery. Plant two varieties for better crops.

Do not feed plants the first year. In succeeding years, use cottonseed meal, ammonium sulfate, or any commercial fertilizer prepared for camellias, azaleas, or rhododendrons.

Care after planting

Blueberries require constant light moisture in the soil, and you can damage their shallow roots by cultivating. For both of these reasons, mulch the plants heavily. Use any organic material such as straw, leaves, peat moss, or a combination, and renew it regularly to keep it about six inches deep. Some materials will use nitrogen as they decay, and you will have to compensate with extra feeding.

Pruning blueberries

The technique is simple, and you don't have to be too precise. Leave the plants alone for two or three seasons, trimming only tangles or broken twigs. Then, to cut back a little on the extremely heavy crops of small berries, remove some of the oldest canes and clip out the weakest twigs. For the largest berries, clip off the outer third to half of the fruiting twigs you retain.

If you never prune you will still get fruit, but it will be small, and eventually decline in quantity.

Pests and disease

Blueberries suffer from very few difficulties, but birds will take them all unless you net the plants. Nurseries carry suitable netting.

Harvest

It's best to taste blueberries before picking, since they tend to be a bit tart up to harvest.

The variety list

Approximately the same varieties are used throughout the country, since the conditions for growing them are so similar.

Early season

'Weymouth.' From New Jersey. The large, round berry has a dark blue skin, little aroma. Best for cooking, but it ripens

Harvest high-bush blueberries from Washington to North Carolina. This cluster grew on 'Dixi' variety.

All those in the pail didn't come from one plant, but blueberries give a good return in small space.

very early. The bush is very productive, erect, and spreading, not vigorous. Available: (2), (4), (31).

'Earliblue.' New Jersey, 1952. One of the best for all areas. The fruit is large, light blue, and firm. The picking scar is small, so fruit keeps well and is resistant to cracking. The plants are upright and comparatively hardy. Available: (2), (6), (7), (14), (36).

'Northland.' Michigan, 1968. A very hardy variety for colder regions. The fruit is medium-sized and round, moderately firm and medium blue. The flavor is good. The plant is spreading, reaching only four feet at maturity. Available: (14), (??).

Midseason

'Collins.' New Jersey, 1959. The fruit is large and light blue, firm and sweet. It resists cracking. The plants are erect, well shaped, and fairly hardy, but not consistent in production. Available: (14), (36).

'Bluecrop.' From New Jersey, 1952. Recommended in all areas. The fruit is large and light blue, rather tart, but an excellent keeper, good in cooking. The fruit stands cold well which recommends the plant for the shortest Michigan growing seasons. The plant is upright and medium hardy. Available: wide distribution.

'Bluehaven.' Michigan, 1968. The fruit is large and light blue, ripening over a long season. The flesh is firm, aromatic, and does not crack. The plant is tall and upright, fairly hardy and consistent. Locally available.

'Blueray.' New Jersey, 1959. The fruit is very large, firm, and sweet. The plant is upright and spreading. A recommended variety in Washington. Available: wide distribution.

'Berkeley.' New Jersey, 1949. The very large fruit is pale blue, firm, resistant to cracking. The bush is fairly upright, moderately hardy. Recommended along the West Coast into Northern California. Available: wide distribution.

'Stanley.' New Jersey, 1930. A widely recommended variety. The medium-sized fruit is firm, with good color and flavor. The bush is hardy, vigorous, upright. Since there are few main branches, pruning is easy. Available: (2), (4), (7), (14), (31).

Late season

'Coville.' New Jersey, 1949. An inconsistent variety with large light blue fruit that remains tart until near harvest. The plant is medium hardy. Available: wide distribution.

'Dixi.' New Jersey, 1936. The name is not an affectionate term for the South. It means "I have spoken" or loosely, "That's my last word." It was given by the developer, F. V. Coville upon his retirement. The fruit is large, aromatic, and flavorful, good fresh. The picking scar is large, so the fruit keeps poorly. The plant is productive, recommended in most areas. Available: (7).

'Jersey.' New Jersey, 1928. Large fruit in a long and loose cluster on a vigorous and spreading plant. It is a preferred commercial variety in Michigan and is recommended on the West Coast. Available: wide distribution.

Birds and kids leave these berries alone until they're ripe.

Grapes

In the earliest periods of human history, four foods were already important. In the cold north there were apples and honey. In the warmer south there were olives and grapes.

All are still important, but grapes stand out from the other three, entering our religion, our poetry, and even our popular phrases: "Peel me a grape"; "Sour grapes"; "The grapes of wrath."

The reason for the great importance of this one fruit is, of course, the juice. Fermented into wine, it provided the only safe drink during the thousands of years when water mysteriously carried disease.

The American grape entered our history more recently than the vine of Europe, but it has already played an important part, since its roots saved the European grape from extinction during the phylloxera plague of the last century. More recently, American grapes have entered into sturdy hybrids that carry European wine grapes far north of their original climate area.

Soil and site

Grapes send their roots very deep if they can. In heavy or shallow soils, you will have to supply the best conditions you can manage at the surface, working in organic matter and mulching the roots. In addition, you should plant in a place where cold air does not gather in spring and fall, and where summer ventilation is good. Otherwise frost and disease will damage vines and fruit.

Planting and early training

See page 95 and 96 for planting and training sketches. Grapes are cut back heavily at planting. After the initial

'Niagara,' good for making white wine, or eating fresh.

training period, American and hybrid grapes differ. See pruning, below.

Pruning

American grapes will not fruit on buds near the main stem. You must leave a long cane during dormant pruning, allowing about 10 buds to remain. This style of pruning is therefore called cane pruning. European hybrids bear fruit on shoots from the buds near the main stem and will overbear if you leave too many buds, so they are pruned to short "spurs" with two buds remaining on each. The method is called spur pruning. Instructions and sketches appear on page 96.

Feeding grapes

Use a complete fertilizer on your vines, and let color and growth rate determine the frequency and amount of application. Vines should have green leaves, not yellow, and should grow well through early summer. Too much fertilizer will force lush growth during the ripening period and may damage the crop on the vine and the buds for the following year.

Harvest

Harvest table grapes by flavor and appearance. When the grapes taste sweet, pick the bunch. (If they never taste sweet, try another variety, or replant near a south wall or south fence corner where the vines get trapped heat.)

Wine grapes are trickier, and homemade wines from garden grapes take lots of trial and error. The sugar level is critical, but tasting doesn't help as much as it might since very acid grapes may taste tart even when they contain sugar. For juice the sugar level is unimportant except as it pleases you personally, so juice is always a safer use for home wine grapes.

Pests and disease

Grapes mildew badly and need a fungicide. The classic remedy is copper sulfate. Various beetles, such as curculio, and aphids may give you trouble. For bird damage, enclose ripening bunches in brown paper bags. Don't use plastic as moisture will collect inside.

The variety list

The American grapes are listed first, with a note when they are choice juice or wine grapes. French hybrids are listed second.

American grapes

'Alden.' New York, 1952. Ripens just before 'Concord.' The large clusters of reddish-black berries are juicy with fine aroma. Skin won't slip. Vine tends to overbear, so thin. Somewhat tender. Available: (2), (3), (27), (28), (32).

'Bath.' New York, 1952. Just after 'Concord.' Medium clusters of black, juicy berries. No 'foxy' American flavor. Vine needs thinning, fairly hardy. Available: (2), (28), (32).

'Buffalo.' New York, 1938. Three weeks before 'Concord.' Wine or juice. The fairly large cluster holds reddish-black fruits with heavy bloom. Slipskin. Vine is vigorous and hardy. Available: wide distribution.

▷

American and European table grapes. You will find at least one variety for any climate except the warm-weather South. There, gardeners use muscadines or selected warm-winter bunch grapes, southern specialties.

Alden

Bath

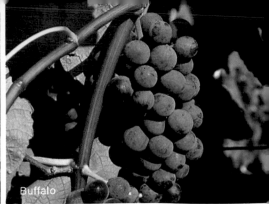

Buffalo

Fredonia

Interlaken Seedless

Lakemont

Golden Muscat

New York Muscat

Romulus

Schuyler

Seneca

Steuben

Tokay

Van Buren

Vinered

Aurora | Baco #1 | Chancellor

The Finger Lakes area of New York and the wine-making area of Ontario now use extensively the grapes pictured here. They are hardy and have many of the characteristics of the fine European varieties. Ohio wine makers also find them satisfactory.

'Catawba.' North Carolina. Just after 'Concord.' Wine or juice. The red berries require a long season to ripen. Thin to hasten development. For southerly areas with longest growing seasons. Ohio wine grape. Available: wide distribution.

'Cayuga White.' Approximately with 'Concord.' The tight clusters of white berries are of high dessert quality. Available: (28).

'Concord.' Massachusetts. This is a late grape, so well known and widely planted that it hardly needs description. The dark blue, slipskin berries have a special flavor that the juice retains after processing. It is often the standard of quality in judging American grapes. The 'Concord' flavor is what is meant by 'foxy.' Available: wide distribution.

'Delaware.' New Jersey. Fifteen days before 'Concord.' Wine and juice. The bunch and berries are small, excellent for dessert and a major wine grape. Vines mildew. Available: (2), (8), (14), (23), (32).

'Fredonia.' New York. Ten days before 'Concord.' This variety should be allowed to set heavily as it sometimes gives difficulty with pollination. This is the top black grape in its season. Vines are hardy. Available: wide distribution.

'Himrod.' New York. Nearly a month before 'Concord.' This is the top white seedless grape throughout northern states. 'Thompson' types replace it where weather is warmer. Brittle vines are only moderately hardy. Available: wide distribution.

'New York Muscat.' New York. Two weeks before 'Concord.' Wine and juice. The reddish-black berries in medium clusters have muscat aroma, which is very rich and fruity, not foxy. Winter injury below −15 degrees. Available: (28), (32).

'Niagara.' Just before 'Concord.' Wine and juice. The most widely planted white grape, more productive than 'Concord.' It is vigorous, moderately hardy. Available: wide distribution.

'Schuyler.' New York. To three weeks before 'Concord.' Berry resembles European grapes in flavor. It is soft and juicy with tough skin. Fairly hardy and disease-resistant. Available: (3), (27), (28).

'Seneca.' New York. Nearly a month before 'Concord.' The small-to-medium berries resemble European grapes, have tender golden skin, sweet and aromatic flavor. Vine is

New York Muscat | Rougeon | Ventura

Chellois

De Chaunac

Foch

hardy, takes cane pruning although one parent is European type. Available: (2), (14), (28).

'Sheridan.' New York. Later than 'Concord.' The large berries have tough black skin, require long season to mature. Concord type. Vines are hardy. Available: (2), (28), (32).

'Steuben.' New York. Ten days before 'Concord.' The blue-black berries grow in medium clusters, are sweet and aromatic. Vine is productive, hardy, disease-resistant. Available: wide distribution.

'Van Buren.' New York. A month before 'Concord.' The small-to-medium clusters of jet-black grapes have sweet, foxy flavor. Earliest of 'Concord' types. Vine is hardy. Available: (2), (3), (14), (20), (23), (28).

'Veeport.' Ontario. Just before 'Concord.' Wine and juice. Medium clusters of black grapes primarily for wine or juice, but acceptable fresh. Vine is vigorous. Available: (28).

French hybrids

Spur-prune these. They are hybrids of European and less known American grapes, not of 'Concord' type *Vitis labrusca* grapes. All are for wine or juice, but good fresh.

'Aurora' (Seibel 5279). A very early white grape that is soft with a pleasant flavor. It is moderately productive, grows far better on sandy soils than heavy ones. Choose it if early ripening is needed. Available: wide distribution.

'Baco #1' ('Baco noir'). This midseason variety produces small clusters of small black grapes. It is extremely vigorous and productive. Available: wide distribution.

'Chancellor' (Seibel 7053). A vigorous blue-fruited variety that ripens in late midseason. The vigorous vines produce well even though they are subject to downy mildew. Available: (2), (28).

'De Chaunac' (Seibel 9549). A midseason variety that is one of the best blues. The clusters are medium to large on vigorous and productive vines. One of the best for home wine making. Available: (2), (6), (14), (27), (28).

'Foch.' A very early black variety that bears clusters of medium size with medium berries. Birds love them, so you will have to protect the crop. Very vigorous vines. Available: (2), (3), (6), (27), (28).

Seyve Villard 12-375. For table use as well as wine. The white berries ripen in late midseason. The vines are vigorous, productive, and hardy. Available: (2), (28).

Seyve Villard 5276. An early variety with large and compact bunches of white berries. It is subject to downy mildew and black rot. Available: (2), (23), (28).

Verdelet

Villard Noir

Currants and gooseberries

As you can see from the photographs here, currants and gooseberries are among the most beautiful of the small fruits, but they are good home-garden shrubs for other reasons as well.

You won't often see fresh fruit in the market, since crops from the limited commercial plantings go to processors for commercial jellies and canned fruits. But since the plants are ornamental, easy to care for and productive, northern gardeners can tuck a few among other shrubs—for the bloom, fruit, and fall color. The crop can be used for jelly and pie, or just fresh eating for those who like a tart fruit.

We discuss only the red and white currants of the species *Ribes sativum,* and the gooseberries, *Ribes grossularia* and *R. hirtellum.* The black currant, *Ribes nigrum,* so aromatic and rich in vitamin C, is unfortunately banned almost everywhere, since it is part of a disease cycle of five-needle pines. The other Ribes species also take part in transferring this disease (the white pine blister rust), and they too are banned in some areas. Ask your nurseryman, and do not transport or plant any currant or gooseberry from outside your region without checking with your Cooperative Extension Office.

Planting

Fall or winter planting is a good idea, since the plants leaf out early. In cold climates, plant right after the leaves drop and the roots will establish before winter. Space the plants about four feet apart, or set them closer if more convenient, but expect them to grow less vigorously. If summer is hot, plant them against a north wall. In most areas, plant in the open, but be sure soil moisture is constant. Set the plants a little deeper than they grew in the nursery.

Feeding and mulching

The plants are heavy feeders and require a regular program of feeding with nitrogen. The leaves will begin to yellow if soil nitrogen level is low. Mulch will help keep weeds down and maintain constant moisture.

Soil

Almost any soil will do, but a rich, well-drained loam is best.

Pruning

No pruning is necessary if you want only light crops on plants that are mainly ornamental. The plants bear the best fruit on the base of stems of the previous season, and on spurs along two-year-old stems. To prune, remove stems that are more than three years old during the dormant season. You can leave 9 to 15 stems, depending upon the age of the plants.

Plants produce for up to 20 years in ideal climates, less in warmer, southerly climates.

Pale American gooseberry reddens up when ripe.

Choose 'White Imperial,' 'White Grape,' among white currants.

Pests and disease

Currants are attacked by the usual aphids, mites, and so on, requiring occasional sprays (or hosing with water for mites). The most serious disease does not affect the currants themselves. Spores of white pine blister rust from miles away spend part of their lives on the currants, then transfer to pines growing within about 300 feet. Currants are banned where there is a white pine timber crop, but check your own and neighbors' gardens for pines with bundles of five needles, and if you find them, don't plant currants.

The variety list

Currants are listed first, then gooseberries. Gooseberry stems are thorny.

Currants

'Perfection.' An old variety with red fruit of medium size in loose clusters. The plant is upright with good foliage, vigorous, and productive. Recommended in Washington and Oregon. Available: wide distribution.

'Red Lake.' Minnesota, 1920. Recommended everywhere that currants will grow. The medium-to-large berries are light red in long, easy-to-pick clusters. The plants are slightly spreading. Highest yield in Canadian trials. Produce well in California. Available: wide distribution.

'Stephens No. 9.' Ontario, 1938. Good Great Lakes variety with fairly large berries of medium red in medium clusters. Plants are spreading and productive. Locally available.

'White Grape.' A white variety that is widely sold, but perhaps surpassed in quality by 'White Imperial' if you can find it. Available: (28), (32).

'Wilder.' Very old variety from Indiana that is still available in the Midwest. The dark red berries are firm but tender, very tart. Plants are large, hardy, and long-lived.

Gooseberries

'Clark.' Ontario. The fruit is large, red when ripe, on plants that are usually free of mildew. Good Canadian variety. Available: (32).

'Fredonia.' New York. The large fruit is dark red when ripe. Plants are productive and vigorous, open growth. Available: (32).

'Oregon Champion.' Oregon. Good variety for all West Coast growing areas. The medium-sized fruit is green. Available: (3), (7), (10), (15).

'Pixwell.' North Dakota, 1932. Very hardy variety for Central and Plains States. The berries hang away from the plant, are easy to pick. The canes have few thorns. Available: wide distribution.

'Poorman.' An American type with red fruit, recommended in the Pacific Northwest and the Central States. The plants are spiny and spreading. Available: (32).

Red currants add extraordinary beauty to the garden.

Easy to grow, red currants make the finest jelly.

Space-saver training

If you have a small garden, forget all the old advice about distances between trees. Fruit can be grown successfully as hedges, garden dividers, boundary plantings, and espaliers. In this chapter, we show you how to crowd a lot of plants in small spaces.

With dwarfing rootstocks and a little training you can confine fruit trees within tiny spaces. The French, for example, grow apples as a foot-high border around beds of vegetables. That technique will work only for cool-climate gardeners, but there are close planting and training methods for mild-climate gardeners as well.

Home gardeners are not the only ones concerned with limited-space-planting these days. Commercial growers are experimenting with training methods that let them grow fruit in hedgerows and harvest their crop without hauling ladders and climbing 30 feet up a standard tree. The methods we outline here combine commercial experience with the training methods that French gardeners call espalier and cordon training. You can be as formal as you like in shaping the plants, but the modern tendency is toward less formal shapes that are easier to achieve and maintain.

Growing fruit in tight spaces is really no harder than maintaining a healthy rosebush, but keep the following points in mind to avoid frustration:

✔Be especially careful about planting and general maintenance. Prepare your soil well and use low raised beds where drainage is a problem. Feed and water on a regular schedule. Spray before damage occurs (some pests and diseases do their work before you can really see the results). Don't let new growth escape from you and spoil the pattern. Look your plants over often.

✔In limited-space planting, training continues at all seasons for the life of the plant. Since the plant is right beside you in the living-space garden, inspecting it is really no chore, but be ready to pinch or snip at any time. Major pruning is still a winter task, but in summer you head or cut away wild growth and suckers, and you may need to loosen or renew ties or add new ones.

◁

Formally espaliered trees like these serve four purposes; they define property boundaries; break up expanses of garden or lawn; enhance the landscape with their aesthetic, spreading branches; and provide generous fruit harvest in a limited space.

How does your tree grow?

Be sure you understand the normal growth pattern of the plant you intend to train. For example, a dwarfed apple or pear tree grows slowly and bears its fruit in the same places for years. The little fruiting twigs, called spurs, may need to be renewed over the years, but you can confine the trees to very formal shapes and keep them there. A peach or nectarine fruits on branches that grew the previous year. Old branches won't bear, so you cut them away like berry canes and replace them with new growth from the base of the tree. This heavy pruning means that rigid patterns are impossible. A peach can be fanned out over a wall or grown as a hedge, but cannot be held to a strict cordon or candelabra shape.

This informally espaliered cherry tree effectively complements the stark vertical lines of the supporting picket fence.

Photographs of variety test plot in Mid-Columbia Experiment Station at Hood River, Oregon. Apples on M.9 root stock were planted 2 feet apart and trained at a 45° angle to induce early fruiting. Bent in this fashion the central leader operates like a lateral branch of a regular orchard tree. The bending increases the number of fruiting spurs. Additional spur development is encouraged by both dormant and summer pruning.

Rootstocks

In the section on dwarfing (pages 12–15) you will see the effects of various dwarfing rootstocks on apple trees. Unfortunately, these stocks are not labelled separately in most retail nurseries, and the salesmen may not be able to tell you what you are buying.

As a general rule, apple varieties sold as dwarf trees will be budded on the rootstocks called Malling 7 and Malling 26, which can produce trees of rather large size if the fruiting variety is vigorous. The smallest trees on these roots will be spur varieties which are already partially dwarfed since they produce shorter branch segments between each fruiting twig, or spur.

Very vigorous fruiting varieties will have to be controlled by more frequent summer pruning. If you find that one tree in a hedge or row regularly overgrows and escapes the pattern you have chosen, you would do well to remove it and plant a less vigorous tree.

How deep to plant

Dwarfing rootstocks cause dwarfing because they are not themselves very vigorous or deep rooted. Trees on the smallest stocks may blow out of the ground unless they have support. Many nurserymen now are placing the bud of the fruiting variety rather high on the rootstock, up to 6 or 8 inches above ground. On the tree you buy, this bud union shows as a bulge with a healed scar on one side. Plant the tree with the union about 2 inches above the soil. This is deeper than it grew in the nursery and accomplishes two things: first, the deep planting makes the tree a little more stable; second, the rootstock is less likely to send up suckers from underground.

Deep planting can be dangerous in poorly drained soil where rot is a problem. If your soil is wet and heavy, use a raised bed or mound to bring the soil *up* to the bud union instead of planting deep.

Be very careful never to bury the bud union in soil or mulch at any time during the life of the tree. If moist

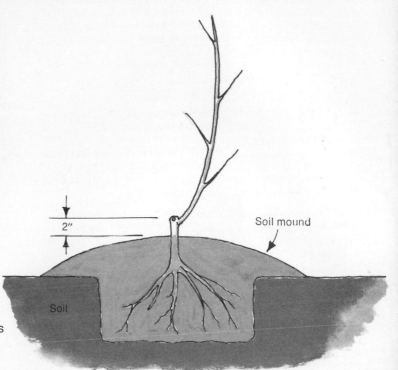

Soil mound

Soil

2″

material touches the union, the upper fruiting part will root and its vigorous root system will produce a full-sized tree instead of the dwarf you bought. Check the bud union frequently for signs of rooting and keep mulches a few inches away from it.

Summer pruning

Summer pruning weakens a plant by removing the leaves that manufacture nourishment. On trees in limited space this pruning is the main means of confining them, since winter pruning has the opposite effect and causes a vigorous burst of spring growth. On the other hand, too much summer pruning can damage a tree. You will learn the proper amount by doing the work, but here are general guidelines.

First, and most important, don't be too timid. You are unlikely to kill your plant, but if the worst should happen, a dwarf replacement tree (trained informally) will grow into place and begin to fruit in a season or two.

In early summer, remove only excessively vigorous sprouts that threaten to take over the tree. These may suddenly shoot out much farther than any other growth. Cut them off at the base. Also, remove any suckers from below the bud union, cutting to the base. Paint large wounds with pruning compound.

When the *new* growth matures and slows its pace, begin snipping it back. The season will vary, depending on weather, your feeding, and watering, but by July you can begin with some branches, finishing up by early September. Cut off all but about four leaves of the current season's growth on each new branch. Then give your trees a last feeding of nitrogen to produce new fruiting wood. Don't thin out branches. You can do that during winter pruning if necessary.

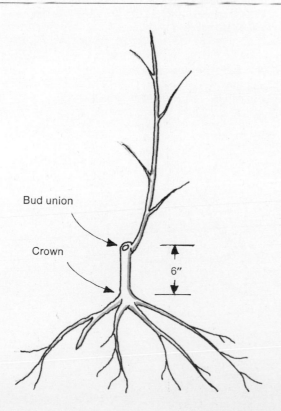

Bud union

Crown

6″

Training to fit your space

You have a broad choice of possibilities in training fruit trees to limited space. Dwarf apples and pears can be trained to formal patterns and still produce fruit, since the flowers and fruit are produced on spurs along old branches. Apricots and European-type plums also produce much fruit on old wood, but since they grow more vigorously they require more of your time to hold a shape. They will not grow or fruit well in rigid patterns. Peaches and nectarines fruit on branches that grew the previous year. You can train them in simple fans or hedges and replace branches that produce fruit with new growth in the fall.

In warm climates you may wish to try training a fig or citrus. The fig fruits twice where the season is long, first on new growth of the previous season then on new growth of the current season. You will lose most of the first crop with severe pruning, but can hope for the second. You can train some citrus (lemons, Rangpur lime) along wires for a fence, or espalier them on walls.

Grapes make good subjects for fences or walls, and a variety that requires a little more heat than your region can offer may produce good fruit when grown on a south or west wall.

You can train cane berries flat against fences or walls, and treat them something like peaches, since you must replace all canes that have fruited with canes of the current season.

The poorest subjects for limited-space training are the quince and cherry. The quince fruits at the tips of new twigs, and the cherry is normally too large to confine and will not fruit at all without a pollinizer close by. Both of these plants can be trained, but your effort is better spent with something more rewarding.

Natural training

Apples and Pears. Both dwarf apples and pears grow and fruit well when trained as hedges against horizontal wires. Use wooden rails in very cold climates. Set posts about 8 feet apart. Stretch a bottom wire between them at 24 inches above ground. If your nurseryman can guarantee Malling 9 rootstocks, place the upper wire at 4 or 5 feet. For Malling 7 or 26 roots, the more common in nurseries, place a third wire at 6 or 7 feet.

Plant the young bareroot trees about 3 feet apart, beginning next to an end post. The last tree will go in about 2 to 3 feet short of the final post. If you buy unbranched trees, bend the trunk, called a whip, at a 45-degree angle and tie it to the wire. If there are any branches with wide crotches, cut them so only two leaf buds remain. Clip off those with narrow crotches at the trunk. Do not feed.

During the first season, train the trunk and any new branches at about 45 degrees, tying loosely where they touch the wires. Pinch off at the tip any branches that seem badly spaced, or that point at right angles to the fence but wait until winter to do this.

The first winter, remove badly placed branches at the trunk. Remove the tips from well-placed branches, cutting to a healthy bud on the top of each branch. Feed lightly as growth begins.

The second summer, continue training shoots at the ends of branches upward at 45 degrees. Cut side growth to four buds beginning in July. Feed again lightly.

Each winter thereafter, remove tangled or damaged growth and cut remaining long shoots to four leaf buds. Feed as growth begins. Each summer, cut out suckers and excessively vigorous sprouts as they appear. Shorten new growth to four leaves from July on, and feed the trees in early August to encourage fruiting wood.

This training method allows side branches to grow outward, away from the fence. Your hedge will eventually become three to four feet wide. You can hold it at that width by pulling some of the outward growth back toward the fence with string, but check ties frequently or they will cut the branches. If parts of your hedge begin to escape and grow too far outward, trim those branches back to healthy side branches in May. To maintain the proper height of five to eight feet, cut top growth back to a healthy side shoot near the top wire in May.

Peaches and nectarines. Since a peach hedge must have its fruiting wood renewed annually, you will need long replacement branches each year. For a hedge, plant as described under apples, using three wires at two, four, and six feet. Cut the whips to about 24 inches long and shorten those side branches that point along the fence to two buds each. Cut off other branches at the trunk. Train all new growth at 45 degrees in both directions. Remove any suckers from below the bud union, cutting to the trunk.

The first winter, cut out about half the new growth at the base, choosing the weakest branches for removal. Cut off the tips of branches you retain if they have grown beyond the hedge limits. Feed lightly as growth begins.

Apple or pear

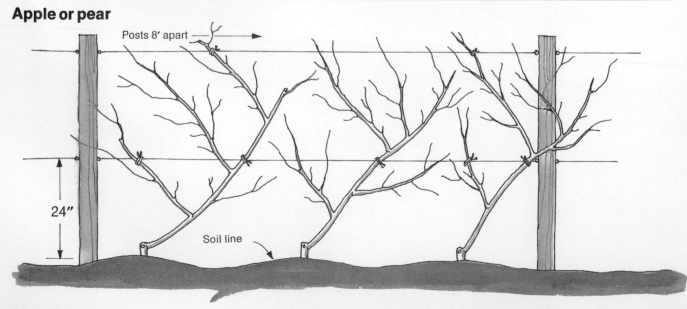

Posts 8' apart

24"

Soil line

Peach

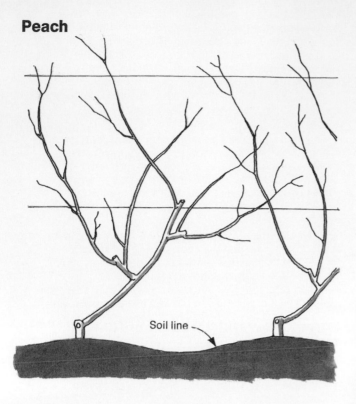

Soil line

Fruit will form on the branches that grew the previous summer. The original trunk and the lowest branch will form an approximate V-shape at or below the lowest wire. During the second summer, choose the healthiest shoots from the lower portions of these main branches, and pinch back all other growth, especially growth above the second wire, after it produces six to eight leaves. The lower shoots will replace the entire upper structure and should be tied back loosely to the fence. Continue to remove suckers below the bud union, and feed lightly twice during early and midsummer.

When leaves drop in fall, cut out all branches that have fruited, and head back the V-shaped main structure to the middle wire. Paint all wounds with pruning compound and train the new growth to the fence. Feed as growth begins. During the summer, again encourage the lower shoots and pinch back the upper growth, feeding twice. Always be sure that new growth is *above* the bud union.

A note on peaches: in parts of the country, the disease known as peach leaf curl attacks both peaches and nectarines each year. If you have this disease in your region, you must spray with a copper fungicide when trees are *dormant,* drenching every branch and twig on all sides. In wet winter climates, spray in fall while the last leaves are still clinging, then again in early winter during a dry spell of at least two days duration.

In drier climates you can wait to apply the first spray until the beginning of winter, and apply the second in midwinter or early spring before the buds swell.

The training method outlined here for a hedge will work well against a wall in cool regions where the wall will supply a little extra heat to ripen fruit. Form a wall-trained tree into a fan shape with the outer branches nearly horizontal, the central branches nearly vertical.

Apricots and plums. Use approximately the same technique described for peaches, but instead of replacing all growth each year, replace about a third and head back new growth on the remaining branches to four to six leaves during the summer.

Fig

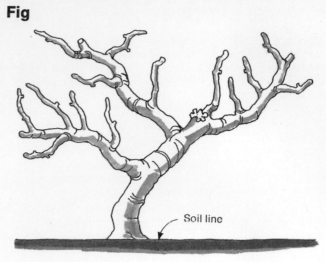

Soil line

Figs. In warm regions where figs grow well, train the young tree to form an irregular, permanent scaffold of trunk plus two to five short branches. These should be headed at two or three feet long, with the trunk at 45 degrees and branches from 45 degrees to horizontal. New growth from these scaffolds should be cut to about 15 inches long in winter and thinned so that the summer hedge is contained at the size you wish. These branches may produce a little fruit in June or July. In summer, trim very lightly to hold the shape. The new summer growth will fruit in fall. Figs are likely to sucker badly and will need attention several times during the growing season.

Where figs can be grown in most years, but freeze back occasionally, grow them as shrubs rather than training them.

Grapes. See grape training methods under Pruning on page 95. A double cordon can be used for fences or against a south or west wall.

Cane Berries. Canes of the previous season can be trained to a fan or column shape against a wall or used as a fence on a two-wire trellis. See cane berries under Pruning, page 97. New canes should be gathered into loosely tied bundles and placed lengthwise along the wall or fence until old canes fruit. After fruiting, cut out old canes and put the new ones in place. Where disease is a problem, as in many areas of the South, cut and destroy all canes immediately after fruiting and use late summer growth for the following year's crop.

Cane berry

Soil line

Formal shapes

Only apples and pears can be trained in formal shapes, and pears may be a disappointment in regions where such diseases as fire blight are a problem. Some formal plants, already trained, are available from nurseries and you can plant these and maintain them with no initial effort, but they will be expensive.

The principle of formal training is simple. You encourage buds to grow at fixed places on a young tree, tie them in position as they lengthen, then hold them in place by light pruning through the year. Malling 7 or Malling 26 rootstocks are fine for formal shapes. Pears will grow on quince rootstock.

A warning on any form of training: ties must be checked frequently, since a tight tie left in place will cut the branch and kill it.

How to encourage bud growth

On any tree, the leaf buds farthest from the ground will grow best. On a horizontal branch, the buds on top will grow best, and those near the trunk will leaf out sooner than those near the tip. In addition, branches grow most vigorously when vertical, and growth slows as a branch is bent toward horizontal.

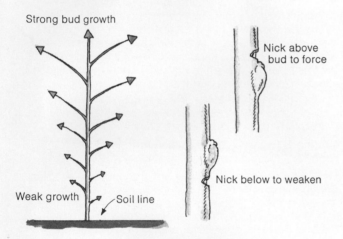

Strong bud growth

Nick above bud to force

Nick below to weaken

Weak growth — Soil line

Cutting a branch forces bud growth below the cut. You can produce a similar effect by cutting a small notch in the bark just above a leaf bud. The bud below the notch will tend to sprout. You can weaken a bud by nicking bark just below it.

Three basic shapes

The three basic shapes that underlie all formal training are: the straight vertical, the 45-degree angle, and the straight horizontal. A single tree is trained in only one shape, but it can be repeated with several branches so that the tree has several vertical, angled, or horizontal members as shown in the sketches. The single members of a formal tree are called *cordons*. A tree trained flat with horizontal cordons is called an *espalier* (used loosely to mean any flattened shape), and a tree trained with angled cordons is called a *palmette*. Vertical training may be adapted to freestanding, three-dimensional shapes.

Training vertical trees

Single cordon. Plant the young tree with the bud union about 2 inches above the soil surface. Cut any side shoots to two buds. The tree may be trained against a wall, pillar, post, or wire trellis, but it must be on the south or west side.

Allow the tree to grow through the first summer with no further pruning. The first winter after planting, cut the central leader back by a third to a half, cutting the minimum amount if side growth is vigorous, more if it has grown weakly. More cutting will force more growth the following summer. New branches should be cut to three buds. New growth on older branches is cut to one bud.

The following summer, beginning in July, cut new branches to three buds, new growth on previously trimmed branches to one bud. Do not cut the top vertical branch until it reaches the height you desire. An exception occurs if the tree fails to produce much side growth. You may then cut new growth on the main stem by a quarter to a third in winter.

When the tree reaches the height you desire, clip the leader about two buds below that height in May. Thereafter, trim all new branches to three buds, and all new growth on old branches to one bud during the summer. In winter, trim any branches you missed earlier. Feed and water carefully to prevent excessive growth.

Forming several vertical cordons

To form a number of vertical cordons on the same tree, you must encourage two or more buds on opposite sides of the trunk, then cut away the trunk above them. To be sure that the right buds grow, you make use of bark notches.

Begin by finding two buds low on the trunk but above the bud union. They should be close together and pointing in opposite directions. Place a horizontal support (wire, wooden rail) an inch or two above the buds. If the support is fixed to a wall, the wall should face south or west.

Just above the lower bud, cut a small notch in the bark. Above the upper bud, nick the bark to the wood. Remove the next two buds entirely, then cut a deep nick in the

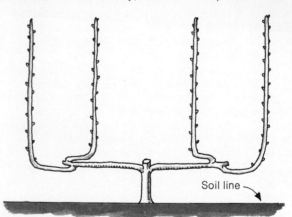

Soil line

bark just *below* the next higher bud. Snip off the trunk above this bud.

The effect will be as follows: the notch and nick above the lowest buds will force them into growth, since nutrients will stop at the cuts. The topmost bud will grow too, but weakly, since you have cut the bark below it. This last bud helps the tree to draw nutrients past the two buds you wish to keep.

In late summer, tie the new shoots from the lower buds to the horizontal support. If one is weaker, let it remain somewhat vertical. In winter, cut the trunk just above the pair of new branches. For a U-shaped double cordon, let the new branches grow vertically again after they form the bottom of the U. After the first season, treat them as you would a single vertical cordon. You can also train the new shoots at 45 degrees or horizontally. Pruning for these shapes is the same as for a vertical cordon.

To form a double U-shape, train the first two shoots into a broad U, becoming vertical when the branches are two feet apart. Let the verticals grow at least two feet up from the bottom support (may require a second season). Repeat the notching and trimming as before on each vertical, training the buds into twin U's one foot across.

Espaliers and palmettes

To form an espalier or palmette with a central trunk and a number of opposing branches you will use a slightly different method. For the first pair of horizontal or angled branches, notch and nick two opposite buds below the

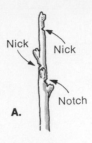

A.

Plant the young tree and set the frame on stakes about 18 inches above the ground. The frame is temporary and may be removed when the training is complete.

Encourage three or four buds about 6 inches below the frame. For three, notch above the first, nick above the second, leave the third alone, then remove the next two and nick below the next. Cut away the trunk above it. Train the shoots horizontally with even spacing

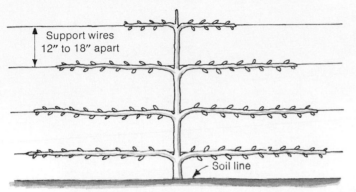

Support wires 12" to 18" apart

Soil line

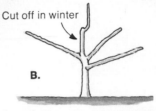

Cut off in winter

B.

In winter, cut away the vertical central stem, leaving the horizontals.

support as before, and remove the next two buds. Do *not* nick the bark below the next bud. You want it to grow strongly to form the central trunk. Cut off the trunk above it. In fall, tie the two lower shoots for an espalier or angled palmette and begin normal summer and winter pruning. Choose two more buds on the central stem for

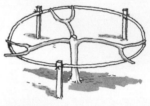

C. Choose buds to form "Y"

On each horizontal, search for two buds about 5 inches away from the center and growing on the sides of the branches, not the top or bottom. Nick the bark beyond the first and cut the branch beyond the second. Remove any buds on the top of the branch nearer the center or they will take over.

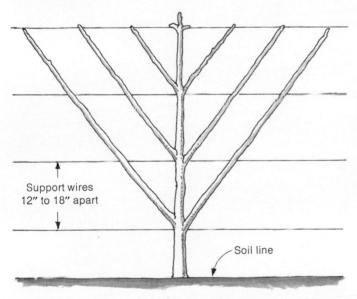

Support wires 12" to 18" apart

Soil line

encouragement, remove the next two, and cut off the trunk above the third. Continue for each pair of horizontals.

Three dimensions

For a three-dimensional shape the technique is the same, but you will encourage three or four closely spaced buds placed evenly around the trunk. Three buds will be divided again for six upright cordons; four buds will produce eight uprights. After shoot growth has begun, you will have to use a hoop or a square frame to train the horizontal portion of your tree. Use a hoop about two feet across for the simple vase shape illustrated. A pointed cone shape will require a hoop three feet across or, for eight verticals, a square frame three feet on a side.

Stake verticals if necessary

D.

When the three pairs grow beyond the hoop, begin training them upward and treat them as ordinary vertical cordons. Trim away any growth on the horizontal portions as soon as you notice it. For four buds the technique is the same, except that you notch the two lower buds, nick the next, and leave the next.

When vertical members reach the height you wish, clip the leader about two buds below that height in May and thereafter trim as described under Training Vertical Trees, page 84.

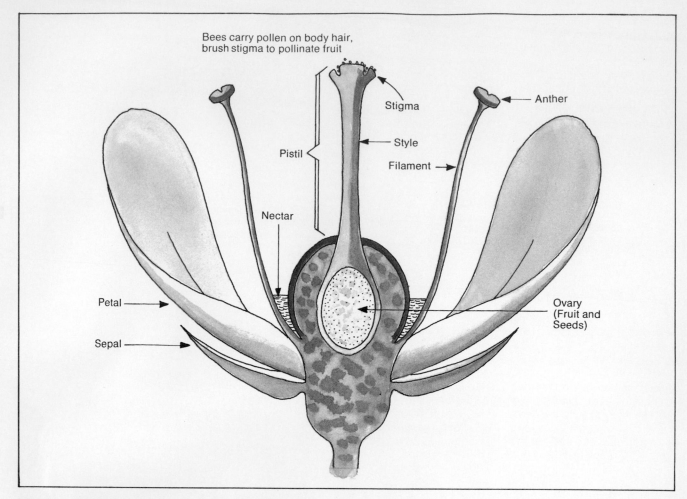

Bees carry pollen on body hair, brush stigma to pollinate fruit

Stigma

Anther

Style

Pistil

Filament

Nectar

Petal

Sepal

Ovary (Fruit and Seeds)

How to achieve proper pollination

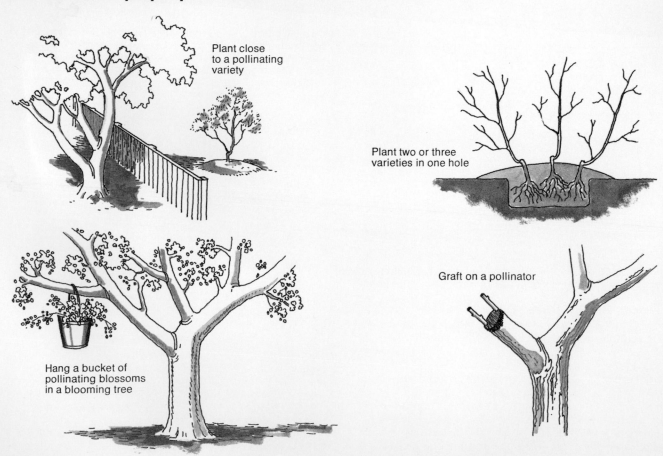

Plant close to a pollinating variety

Plant two or three varieties in one hole

Hang a bucket of pollinating blossoms in a blooming tree

Graft on a pollinator

Pollination, Pruning, and Grafting

**Make the most of your fruit garden by understanding its nature.
How does spring bloom mature into a summer crop?
How can you best train a young plant for strength and abundant fruit?
How can you ripen many varieties on a single tree? Your answers follow.**

Plant breeding may seem like a subject that only a bush or a botanist could love, but every time you bite into an apple or a peach you're tasting the results of breeding. As a general rule, the fruit is only there because the seed has been fertilized.

What should you know?

You may feel that once you plant a tree you've done your part, and the rest is up to it. That idea can lead to fruitless fruit trees. Before you ever lift a shovel, you'll need to understand a little of how fruit is produced.

With a few exceptions (certain figs, for example), fruit will not form unless pollen from the male parts of a flower is transferred to the receptor of the female part. Most of the transferring for the fruits discussed in this book is done by bees. Even when you see bees at work, though, you may not get a crop. The pollen they carry must be of the right sort. Apple pollen, for example, will never pollinize a pear blossom, but more important, apple pollen won't always pollinize an apple blossom.

The right combinations

Some plants are called *self-fruitful.* This means that their blossoms can be fertilized by pollen from another flower on the same tree, or from another tree of the same kind. Self-fruitful plants will produce fruit if they are planted far from any other plant of their kind.

Even self-fruitful plants sometimes give more fruit if another plant of a different variety grows close by. Among the self-fruitful plants are many apples, most peaches and apricots, and the citrus group. Sour cherries are also self-fruitful.

Other plants set fruit only when they receive pollen from a plant of some other variety. Their own pollen is often entirely sterile. Many apples, cherries, and plums fall into this group. The Napoleon (Royal Ann) sweet cherry needs another cherry tree with fertile pollen within at least 100 feet of it, or it bears no fruit. The

individual entries for each fruit in this book will tell you the right combination of plants for a crop.

Never assume that because you have a bearing fruit tree you can be sure of a crop on a new tree of a different variety. Check the entry on that variety for good pollinizers. Plants must bloom at about the same time for cross-pollination to be successful, so a very early apple with sterile pollen needs another early apple as a pollinizer. A late-bloomer may not work well even if its pollen is fertile.

Some plants bear male and female flowers on separate trees. Figs and persimmons are among these. Fortunately, most figs and persimmons available to the home gardener will produce fruit without pollination. If, by some chance, you have a Calimyrna fig tree or an American persimmon in the garden, you will get no fruit unless the tree is female and has been pollinated.

Planting for pollination

A fruit plant that needs a pollinizer needs it close by. The maximum recommended distance is 100 feet between plants, but the closer the better. This is because the bees that do the pollen carrying must fly back and forth between the plants, and they won't if the distance is too great. If your neighbor has a pollinizing variety across the back fence you're in good shape. If not, do one of the following: 1. Plant two trees fairly close together; 2. Plant two to four trees of the same kind in a single planting hole; 3. Graft a branch of a variety with fertile pollen onto a tree that needs pollination.

Sometimes, even though a good pollinizer is close to the tree that needs it and blooms at the same time the bees are uncooperative and your crop is poor. If this happens, trick the bees by gathering a bouquet of flowers with fertile pollen and placing them in a vase of water in the branches of the second tree. Do it early in the morning when the bees are working hard and the temperatures are fairly low.

Common sense pruning

Don't expect to take this book out to your garden, stand in front of your unpruned fruit tree, and know exactly what cuts to make.

You have probably read several publications on pruning and have found that no sketch or photograph of a tree looks exactly like yours.

There is only one way to free yourself from pruning fear or frustration. Just do it!

You need only keep two objectives in mind:
   Cut to create a strong scaffold.
   Cut to admit light to leaves and fruit.

The leaves of the tree produce the sugars which are stored in the fruit. Leaves grow where they receive light.

A properly pruned tree will produce fruit throughout the tree—on low and interior branches. An unpruned tree produces fruit on the light-exposed branch tips.

Use the gentle approach. First cut off poorly placed or weak branches leaving the best ones to grow. If you make a mistake, it's normally self-correcting. The plant will send out new growth to replace what you remove.

So, if the tree needs shaping or reshaping, make the necessary cuts—without fear.

But you need guidelines to select a shape to aim for. We hope to give you the necessary guidelines in these pages. But, be flexible, there are many ways to reach the final objective—fruit.

Pruning and growth

Pruning has a direct effect on the growth of a plant. If you cut part of a bare branch in winter or early spring, the remaining piece will grow more vigorously, producing several shoots for every one you cut. On the other hand, if you cut leafy branches in late summer or fall, you weaken the plant (the missing leaves can't produce food for growth). New growth will follow, but it is less vigorous. In general then, winter pruning stimulates new growth, summer pruning controls a plant.

The illustrations below will help you to recognize the various parts of a plant so that you know what to look for when you go out with clippers and saw.

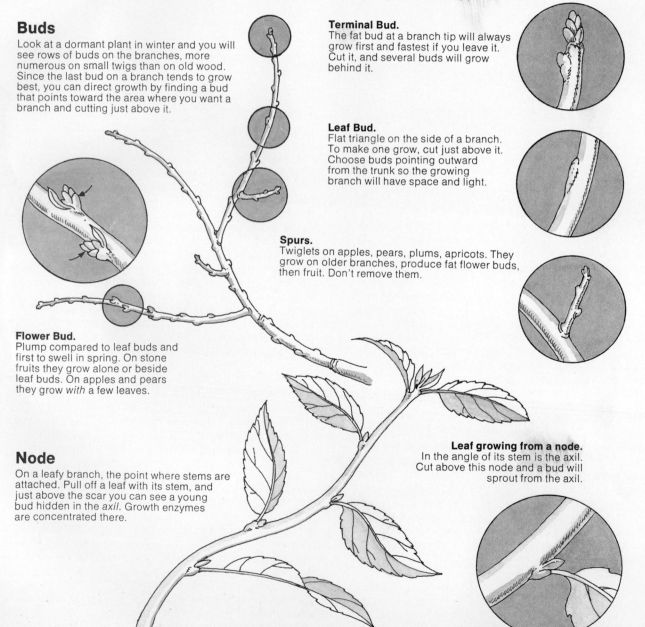

Buds
Look at a dormant plant in winter and you will see rows of buds on the branches, more numerous on small twigs than on old wood. Since the last bud on a branch tends to grow best, you can direct growth by finding a bud that points toward the area where you want a branch and cutting just above it.

Flower Bud.
Plump compared to leaf buds and first to swell in spring. On stone fruits they grow alone or beside leaf buds. On apples and pears they grow *with* a few leaves.

Node
On a leafy branch, the point where stems are attached. Pull off a leaf with its stem, and just above the scar you can see a young bud hidden in the *axil*. Growth enzymes are concentrated there.

Terminal Bud.
The fat bud at a branch tip will always grow first and fastest if you leave it. Cut it, and several buds will grow behind it.

Leaf Bud.
Flat triangle on the side of a branch. To make one grow, cut just above it. Choose buds pointing outward from the trunk so the growing branch will have space and light.

Spurs.
Twiglets on apples, pears, plums, apricots. They grow on older branches, produce fat flower buds, then fruit. Don't remove them.

Leaf growing from a node.
In the angle of its stem is the axil. Cut above this node and a bud will sprout from the axil.

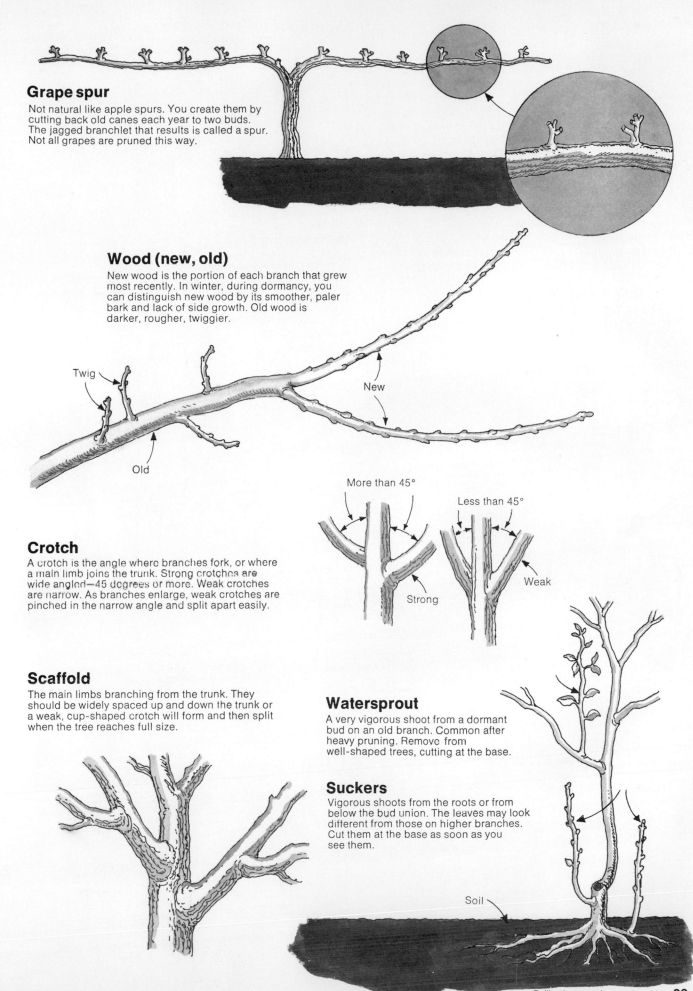

Grape spur

Not natural like apple spurs. You create them by cutting back old canes each year to two buds. The jagged branchlet that results is called a spur. Not all grapes are pruned this way.

Wood (new, old)

New wood is the portion of each branch that grew most recently. In winter, during dormancy, you can distinguish new wood by its smoother, paler bark and lack of side growth. Old wood is darker, rougher, twiggier.

Twig

Old

New

More than 45°

Less than 45°

Crotch

A crotch is the angle where branches fork, or where a main limb joins the trunk. Strong crotches are wide angled—45 degrees or more. Weak crotches are narrow. As branches enlarge, weak crotches are pinched in the narrow angle and split apart easily.

Strong

Weak

Scaffold

The main limbs branching from the trunk. They should be widely spaced up and down the trunk or a weak, cup-shaped crotch will form and then split when the tree reaches full size.

Watersprout

A very vigorous shoot from a dormant bud on an old branch. Common after heavy pruning. Remove from well-shaped trees, cutting at the base.

Suckers

Vigorous shoots from the roots or from below the bud union. The leaves may look different from those on higher branches. Cut them at the base as soon as you see them.

Soil

Making a cut

When you cut away parts of a plant, you leave a wound where pests or disease organisms can enter. To avoid trouble, try to make wounds as small as possible, and protect them until they heal if they are over a half inch in diameter.

The smallest possible wound is made when you remove a bud or twig. If a new sprout grows in toward the trunk, or threatens to tangle with another branch when it's longer, pinch it off right away and save pruning later. If you see the bud of a sucker down near the soil, rub it off with your thumb.

Make your cuts close to a node. The branches grow only at these nodes, and if you cut between them, the stub will die and rot. Cut at a slight angle so no straight shoulder is left to attract disease or burrowing pests.

Do major pruning in early spring, just as the buds swell. New growth will begin to heal the cuts immediately.

Removing a stub

Never leave a projecting stub. It will rot and can damage the branch it is attached to. Cut stubs close to the trunk at a point where the wound will be about the same diameter as the branch you cut. Cutting *very* close leaves a larger wound.

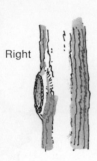

Right

Wrong

Angle your cut

Cut at an angle about ¼ inch above a bud or leaf. As the bud grows, new bark will cover the raw wood.

Cutting a big limb

When you remove a big branch, first undercut at a short distance from the trunk (A). Then saw off the branch beyond the undercut (B). Finally, cut the stub close to the trunk (C). This technique will prevent a falling branch from tearing the bark. Paint the wound with a pruning compound.

B

2"-4"

A

12"

C

Well-healed cut

New tissue grows from the edge of a wound toward the center. If your cut was smooth, the scar will close evenly with a dimple in the very center.

Tools

Illustrated here are the main pruning tools: You should buy 1) quality shears, 2) a lopper for larger branches, 3) a saw for very large cuts. (Saws may be folding, straight, or with replaceable blades.), 4) a large rasp, 5) pole saw and pole pruner. Have shears and loppers sharpened every year, and never force them through too large a branch. You will also need pruning compound and pruning paint to protect fresh cuts.

You may find a large rasp handy for evening up rough edges and smoothing off shoulders. You can rent or buy pole saw and pole pruner for cutting high branches without climbing.

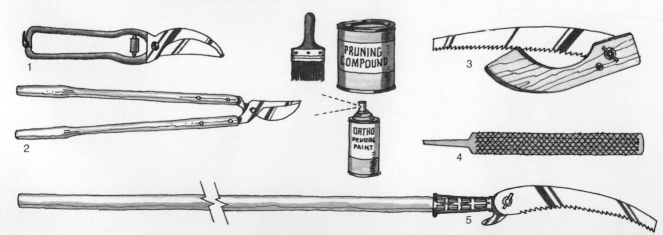

PRUNING COMPOUND

ORTHO PRUNING PAINT

1

2

3

4

5

Starting right

When you first plant a young bareroot tree it will consist of a thin vertical shoot, called a whip, and possibly some twiggy side branches. You must cut it back immediately to balance the loss of root system cut away when the tree was uprooted—remaining roots cannot maintain the whole top. Then too, cutting forces more vigorous growth and you will have a better choice of branches the following winter when you choose your scaffold. Partial exceptions to the rule are certain espaliers (See page 85).

A young tree's calendar goes like this: First dormant season means the first winter after planting, about a year after you bought the tree. Second dormant season is the next winter, two years from purchase. In these first two dormant periods you will prune fairly heavily to establish a sturdy framework. It is best to prune as lightly as possible after that. The tree will grow faster and bear younger if you leave all but a few tangled twigs intact. Apples and pears will require the least pruning up to maturity, apricots and plums a little more, and peaches the most. When a tree reaches bearing age, pruning consists of maintaining the form you have already established.

Shaping young trees

From the first dormant season, you are aiming toward a mature tree of a certain shape. With fruit trees there are two possibilities, the vase shape and the central-leader shape. There are advantages to each, but the modern tendency is to vase pruning.

Vase Pruning. The mature tree will have a short trunk and then spread outward with three or four main limbs. These in turn will branch outward with five to seven secondary limbs. The center of the tree is open so that light penetrates and encourages fruit on the lower branches. This shape is always used with apricots, plums, and peaches, often used with pears and apples.

Central Leader. As the name implies, the mature tree will have a central trunk with a number of major limbs branching outward at various levels. The center of the tree is shaded and produces little or no fruit, and the tree will be tall and hard to prune. On the other hand, it tends to be very strong, holding the weight of a crop well and standing up to weather.

Central-leader pruning is still used for the smallest dwarf apples in a variation called the spindle bush. Since the tree is tiny, shade and pruning are not a problem. Another technique, called delayed-open-center, combines some of the strength of a central trunk with the sunny center of a vase shape. The trunk is allowed to grow vertically until it reaches 6 to 10 feet, then clipped to a side branch.

We recommend the vase shape and describe it below, but also include a description of spindle-bush training (page 92) for dwarf apples on Malling 9 rootstock.

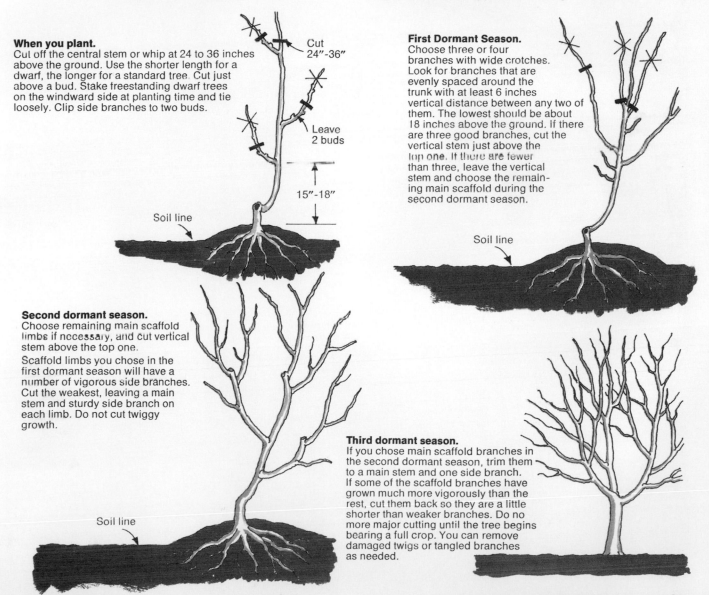

When you plant.
Cut off the central stem or whip at 24 to 36 inches above the ground. Use the shorter length for a dwarf, the longer for a standard tree. Cut just above a bud. Stake freestanding dwarf trees on the windward side at planting time and tie loosely. Clip side branches to two buds.

Cut 24"-36"

Leave 2 buds

15"-18"

Soil line

First Dormant Season.
Choose three or four branches with wide crotches. Look for branches that are evenly spaced around the trunk with at least 6 inches vertical distance between any two of them. The lowest should be about 18 inches above the ground. If there are three good branches, cut the vertical stem just above the top one. If there are fewer than three, leave the vertical stem and choose the remaining main scaffold during the second dormant season.

Soil line

Second dormant season.
Choose remaining main scaffold limbs if necessary, and cut vertical stem above the top one.
Scaffold limbs you chose in the first dormant season will have a number of vigorous side branches. Cut the weakest, leaving a main stem and sturdy side branch on each limb. Do not cut twiggy growth.

Soil line

Third dormant season.
If you chose main scaffold branches in the second dormant season, trim them to a main stem and one side branch. If some of the scaffold branches have grown much more vigorously than the rest, cut them back so they are a little shorter than weaker branches. Do no more major cutting until the tree begins bearing a full crop. You can remove damaged twigs or tangled branches as needed.

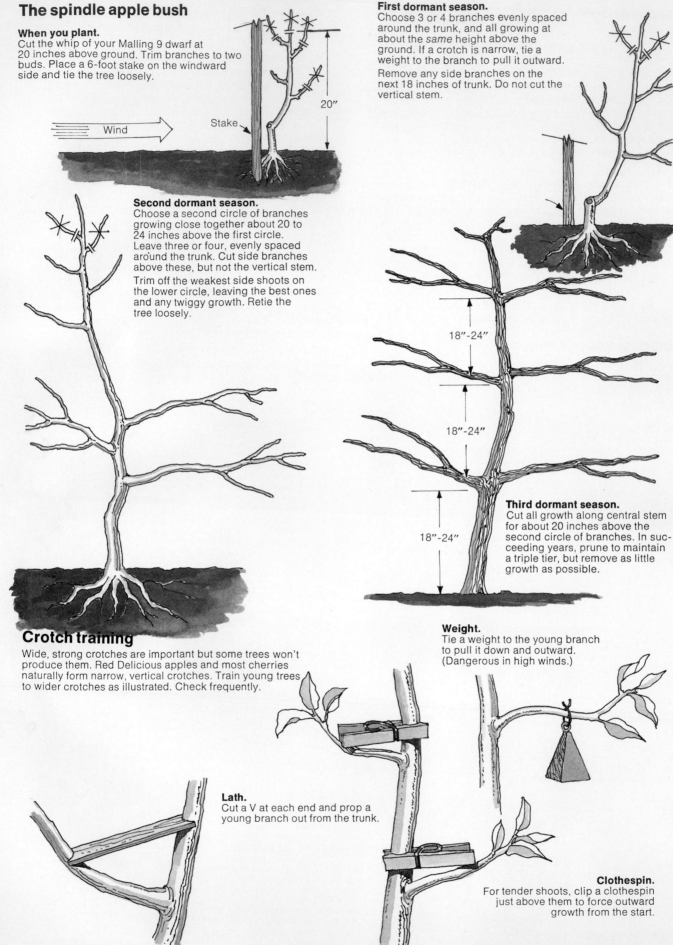

The spindle apple bush

When you plant.
Cut the whip of your Malling 9 dwarf at 20 inches above ground. Trim branches to two buds. Place a 6-foot stake on the windward side and tie the tree loosely.

Wind

Stake

20"

First dormant season.
Choose 3 or 4 branches evenly spaced around the trunk, and all growing at about the *same* height above the ground. If a crotch is narrow, tie a weight to the branch to pull it outward.

Remove any side branches on the next 18 inches of trunk. Do not cut the vertical stem.

Second dormant season.
Choose a second circle of branches growing close together about 20 to 24 inches above the first circle. Leave three or four, evenly spaced around the trunk. Cut side branches above these, but not the vertical stem.

Trim off the weakest side shoots on the lower circle, leaving the best ones and any twiggy growth. Retie the tree loosely.

18"-24"

18"-24"

18"-24"

Third dormant season.
Cut all growth along central stem for about 20 inches above the second circle of branches. In succeeding years, prune to maintain a triple tier, but remove as little growth as possible.

Crotch training

Wide, strong crotches are important but some trees won't produce them. Red Delicious apples and most cherries naturally form narrow, vertical crotches. Train young trees to wider crotches as illustrated. Check frequently.

Weight.
Tie a weight to the young branch to pull it down and outward. (Dangerous in high winds.)

Lath.
Cut a V at each end and prop a young branch out from the trunk.

Clothespin.
For tender shoots, clip a clothespin just above them to force outward growth from the start.

Each fruit is different

Although early training of fruit trees is similar, the growth habit of each kind is different. Apples and pears grow relatively slowly and produce fruit on short spurs along the old branches. The spurs produce for as long as 10 years. Spur-type apples and pears sprout more productive spurs per foot of branch and grow more slowly than ordinary trees.

Cherries produce fruit on spurs, but their main branches may shoot up into long poles. These can be headed back in the first years to encourage branching. Otherwise, cherries need less pruning than other fruit.

Apricots, plums, and prune-type plums grow spurs, but also send out vigorous new shoots at branch tips and need heading and thinning.

Peaches and nectarines produce fruit on new wood of the previous season. They need severe pruning to force new wood.

Remember that . . .

Any heavily pruned tree sends out lots of new growth in spring. If a tree bears on older wood, you will cut back fruit production by heavy pruning. If it bears on new wood, you will stimulate production in the season after the *following* winter.

Pruning always removes *some* fruiting wood. An unpruned tree may bear too heavily, producing small fruit and next to no new growth. Pruning evens the crops over many seasons.

Apples, pears, prune type plums

Trim lightly to remove tangled branches or damaged wood. Cut dangling limbs or vertical watersprouts at base. Head back branch tips to maintain size of older trees. Leave twiggy spurs for fruit production.

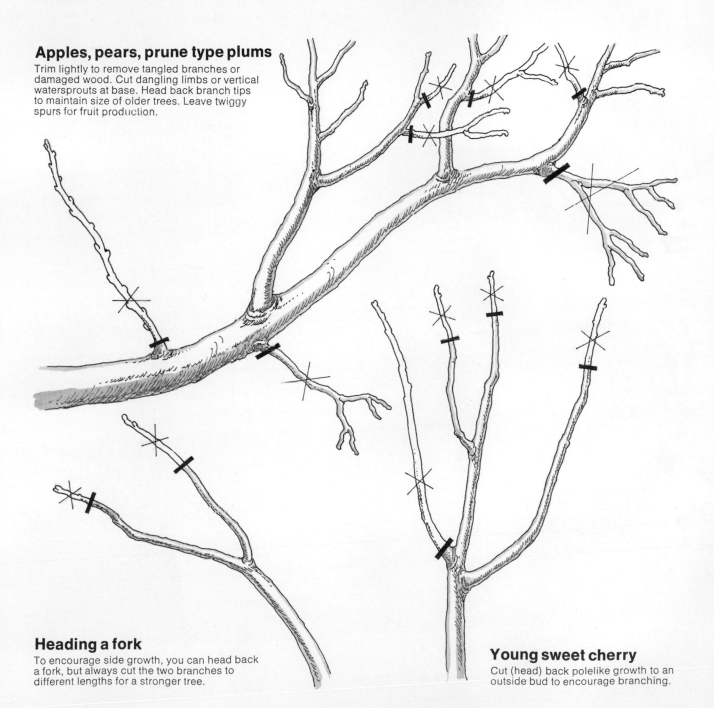

Heading a fork

To encourage side growth, you can head back a fork, but always cut the two branches to different lengths for a stronger tree.

Young sweet cherry

Cut (head) back polelike growth to an outside bud to encourage branching.

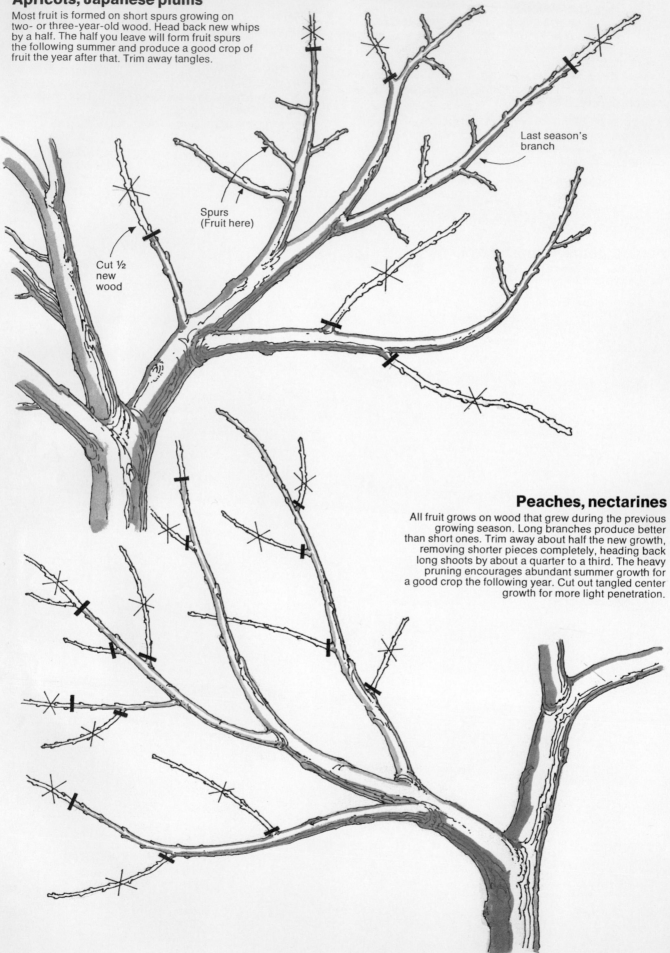

Apricots, Japanese plums

Most fruit is formed on short spurs growing on two- or three-year-old wood. Head back new whips by a half. The half you leave will form fruit spurs the following summer and produce a good crop of fruit the year after that. Trim away tangles.

Last season's branch

Spurs
(Fruit here)

Cut ½
new
wood

Peaches, nectarines

All fruit grows on wood that grew during the previous growing season. Long branches produce better than short ones. Trim away about half the new growth, removing shorter pieces completely, heading back long shoots by about a quarter to a third. The heavy pruning encourages abundant summer growth for a good crop the following year. Cut out tangled center growth for more light penetration.

Grapes—what kind do you have?

All grapes require heavy pruning to produce fruit, but different kinds need different pruning. Wine grapes and muscadines will usually need spur pruning in which all side branches of a mature plant are cut to two buds in fall or winter. Two new shoots grow on the spur you leave, and each produces a cluster or bunch of fruit.

Some grapes do not produce fruit on shoots that grow too near the main scaffold. Thompson Seedless and many American grapes such as Concord are among these. For these grapes you must cane-prune. Instead of cutting to a short spur in winter, leave two whole canes from the previous growing season. When fruit forms from side growth along this cane, clip the cane off beyond the next set of leaves. At the same time, you encourage two new canes that will bear fruit the following year.

Both spurs and canes grow from a permanent trunk or trunk plus arms that you train on a trellis or arbor.

The variety list from page 68 on indicates whether you should practice spur or cane pruning on a listed variety. In general, all muscadines need spur pruning. Americans of the Concord or "foxy" group take cane pruning. Grapes of the wine-producing sort usually will take spur pruning. For any grape not listed, inquire at your Cooperative Extension Office, or experiment by cane-pruning a portion of a mature vine, spur-pruning another portion.

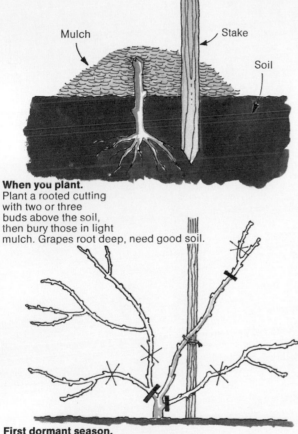

When you plant.
Plant a rooted cutting with two or three buds above the soil, then bury those in light mulch. Grapes root deep, need good soil.

First dormant season.
Choose the best shoot and cut others to the base. Head remaining shoot to 3 or 4 strong buds.

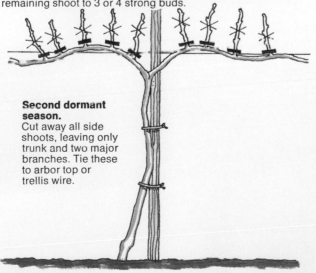

Second dormant season.
Cut away all side shoots, leaving only trunk and two major branches. Tie these to arbor top or trellis wire.

First growing season.
Leave the plant alone. It will grow a number of shoots.

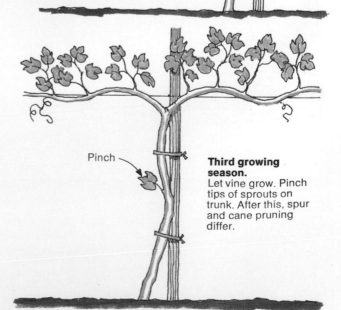

Second growing season.
When new shoots reach about 12 inches long, select the most vigorous and pinch off others at the trunk. Tie remaining shoot to a support (arbor post, trellis post). When the shoot reaches branching point at arbor top or trellis wire, pinch it to force branching. Let two strong branches grow, pinch any others at 8 to 10 inches long.

Third growing season.
Let vine grow. Pinch tips of sprouts on trunk. After this, spur and cane pruning differ.

Shapes for vines

You have a choice of arbor training, cordon training, head training, or trellised canes. An arbor is an overhead frame on posts at least seven feet tall.

The overhead portion should be at least eight to ten feet on a side. Train a vine up each vertical post with two branches crossing the top horizontally. It may take more than two seasons to reach the top and begin training the horizontals.

A cordon is a horizontal permanent branch on a wall or trellis. Train each vine to either two or four cordons. For four, allow three shoots to grow during the second growing season. Train two of the shoots horizontally, tie the other vertically until it reaches the upper support then pinch and select two horizontals.

A head-trained vine is free-standing but may not give you much fruit. This method is attractive and you can use it for spur or cane grapes. Stake the young trunk and allow up to four shoots to grow, beginning about 24 inches above the ground or higher. To spur-prune, cut each shoot to two buds in winter each year. To cane-prune, gather the fruiting canes upward and tie them together toward the tip. Let growth from renewal buds trail.

Trellised canes are grown on wire like a four-arm cordon, but the permanent wood is confined to short stubs near the trunk and the fruiting canes are tied to the wire.

Third dormant season: spur pruning

Remove all shoots from vertical trunk. Choose the strongest side shoots on horizontal branches and cut to two buds. Remove weak shoots at base, spacing two-budded spurs about 6 to 10 inches apart.

Annual.
Each dormant season after this, each spur will have a pair of shoots that produced fruit during the summer. Cut the stronger to two buds. These buds will produce fruit-bearing shoots in summer. Remove weaker shoot. Repeat each year. Always keep trunk clear of growth.

Cut

Tie

Cut

Tie

Third dormant season: cane pruning

Remove shoots from trunk. Cut horizontal branches back so that two long shoots remain on each. On a two-wire trellis, you can leave up to eight shoots per vine. Tie the shoot farthest from the trunk to the trellis. Cut the other to 2 or 3 buds. The tied shoot will fruit the following summer. The clipped shoot will produce growth to replace it next winter, fruit the year after.

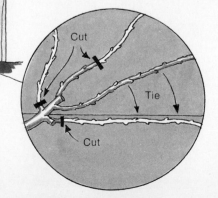

Cut

Tie

Cut

Annual.
When outside cane has borne fruit, cut it back to the inside stub, now holding two or three new canes. Select the best and tie it to the trellis for fruit. Cut the next to two or three buds. Remove the weakest at the base. Repeat each year.

Cane berries and bush berries

All cane berries fall into two groups: those with rigid canes that grow upright, and those with trailing canes that tend to creep. Both types produce fruit on canes that sprouted the previous year. Cut these canes to the ground as soon as you have harvested the crop. Leave about eight of the best new canes, cutting the rest. Everbearing raspberries differ slightly in that a light crop forms at the top of new canes in fall. Cut only the portion that fruits. The lower portion will bear the following year.

Rigid-caned berries. (Blackberry, blackcap raspberry, purple raspberry.) Cut old canes after fruit harvest. Pinch young blackberry canes when they reach 36 inches; pinch blackcaps and purple raspberries at 24 to 30 inches. Pinched canes will send out lateral growth. In winter, cut blackberry laterals to 15 to 18 inches, raspberries to 10 to 12 inches. Paint the bases white to distinguish them from summer growth. If you wish, tie the erect canes to a single wire, stretched at 18 inches above ground.

Trailing Raspberries. For single-crop berries, cut canes as soon as harvest is over. Train new canes to a post, vertical wire, or to horizontal supports. In summer, as new canes grow, gather them in bunches, tie very loosely, and lay them along the ground until time for training.

For everbearing raspberries, cut canes that fruit early in the season and train young canes. These will fruit at the top in fall. Cut the fruiting portion after harvest but leave the rest.

Trailing blackberries (dewberries). You can treat blackberries like raspberries, although canes are longer and more vigorous. Or try this method: stretch a wire 36 inches above the row of berry plants. After harvest, remove old canes and cut new ones off at 48 inches. Canes that sprawl left are then pulled back to the right side of the wire. Canes that grow right are pulled to the left side. Tie if necessary. Extremely long laterals will grow outward, knitting together. Train them as needed along the wire.

Shrubby fruit plants

The shrubby fruit plants such as currants, gooseberries, and blueberries tend to bear very heavily if left completely unpruned. You can clean them up by removing the oldest shoots, those three and four years old, in winter, and thinning out the worst tangles among the twigs. You need not be too conscientious. If berries are very small one year, thin the following winter. If they are large, skip the thinning.

If you grow elderberries, mahonia, or other berry plants, the same rules apply. Thin tangles if they're bad, and remove the oldest growth if the plant needs thinning.

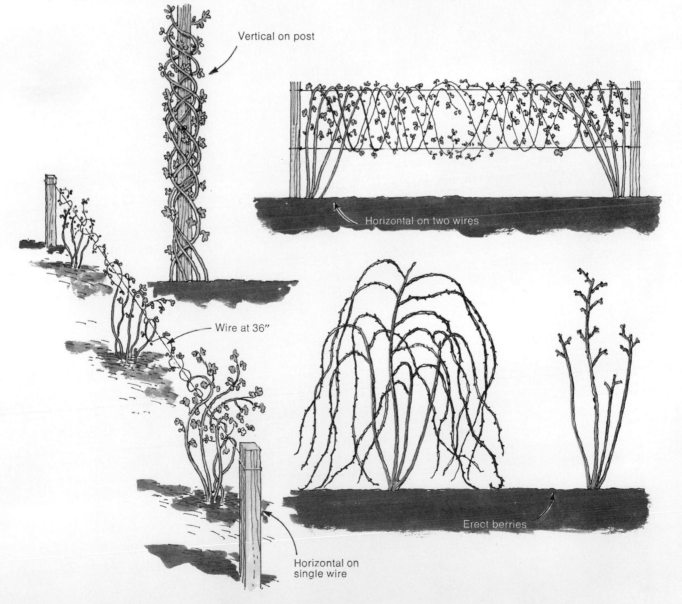

Vertical on post

Horizontal on two wires

Wire at 36"

Horizontal on single wire

Erect berries

Grafting is easy

Grafting lets you take full advantage of limited garden space. A grafted tree can bear up to four or five varieties of fruit, and pollination is much improved when a pollinizing branch grows on the same tree with a variety that needs its pollen.

You can, of course, plant up to four young trees in the same hole with the same space-saving advantages of a grafted plant, but if you inherit a full-grown tree this technique won't do, while grafting is still possible.

Nurseries occasionally sell trees that already bear a number of varieties, but they are likely to be very expensive, and the mixture may not be what you would choose for yourself. Fortunately, grafting is not much more difficult than rooting a cutting, and some methods do next to no damage to the tree even if you fail the first time.

Grafting terms

Understanding terms is important to any skill, and especially important to grafting. The four basic terms involved are *cambium, scion* (SIGH-un), *stock,* and *callus.*

Cambium. This is the growing layer of most garden plants, lying between the bark and the woody portion of a trunk or stem. When you graft a new branch to an old plant the cambium layers of the two pieces must touch.

Scion. This is the new shoot or branchlet that you will attach to an existing plant.

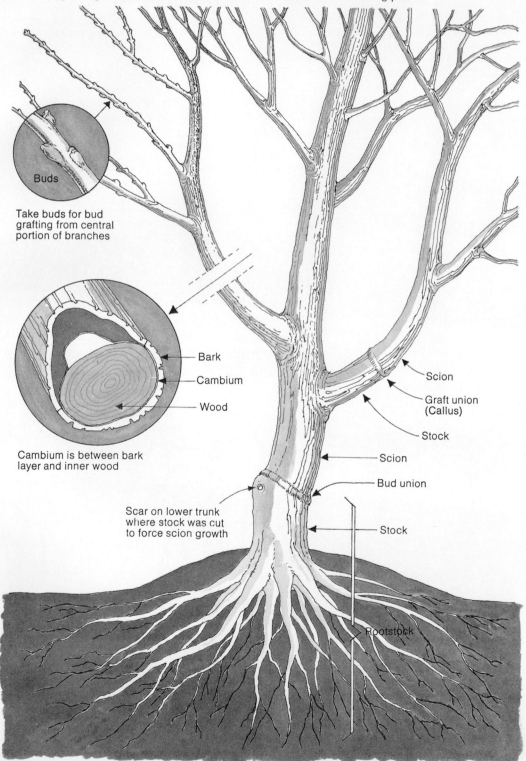

Take buds for bud grafting from central portion of branches

Bark

Cambium

Wood

Cambium is between bark layer and inner wood

Buds

Scion

Graft union (Callus)

Stock

Scion

Bud union

Stock

Scar on lower trunk where stock was cut to force scion growth

Rootstock

Stock. The stock, or rootstock, is the existing plant to which you attach a scion. Scion and stock must usually be closely related, for example pear on pear or apple on apple, but this is not invariably true. (See "Grafts you can Try" following.)

Callus. Both scion and stock grow a mass of special cells as they join together. It is these new cells, called *callus,* that form the actual joint. Callus cells grow best at temperatures above 55 degrees Fahrenheit, and when the plants are active, so grafting is usually done when spring growth is beginning. A special form of grafting called *budding* is possible in summer or fall.

Why graft?

Tree fruits do not, as a general rule, reproduce themselves from seed. Seedlings bear fruit that is different and usually inferior. The only way to grow a new Golden Delicious or Winesap is to graft a piece of the tree to an apple rootstock. Young nursery trees show the graft as a kind of lump on the lower trunk called the bud union.

Grafting can increase the number of varieties you grow at home. If you have space for only one apple tree, you can graft new varieties onto some of its branches. If you do this kind of grafting, match the growth habits of stock and scion. A very vigorous apple branch grafted to a slow-growing spur-type tree may take over and shade out the other branches.

You can also use grafting to correct mistakes. Perhaps you inherit a fruit tree that does poorly in your area for some reason. Instead of replanting, graft on a better fruit. You'll have a crop much sooner than by starting over. Or perhaps your garden tree won't bear because it needs a pollinizer. Graft in a branch of the proper variety and you'll have a good crop and two kinds of fruit.

Nurserymen use grafting to produce trees of smaller-than-normal size. Special roots that slow growth are grafted to desirable varieties of apples, pears, and other fruit, and the resulting trees stay small. You may want to try your hand at this form of grafting in order to save space. The easiest way is to buy a dwarf or semidwarf tree and add varieties of similar growth habit, but you can also propagate new rootstocks from suckers. We discuss dwarfing rootstocks below.

What equipment do you need?

There is much special grafting equipment available, but a home gardener can make do with a sharp pocket knife, a good pair of pruning shears, a roll of plastic electrician's tape (the kind that stretches), and a can of water-base asphalt tree sealer. You may want to add a small cleaver, a hammer and nails, and a pruning saw for grafting larger limbs.

Grafts you can try

Usually you are safe in grafting any apple variety onto an apple stock, or any other fruit onto a tree that bears the same kind of fruit. There are odd exceptions. Peach scions, for example, often join better on almond stock than onto peach stock, and any stone fruit like the peach, plum, or apricot is a bit trickier than the pome fruits such as apples and pears. For any graft, be sure the scion is pointed in the *right direction.* Notice the position of the buds when you cut your scions, and position the graft so that they point the same way, away from the trunk.

Graft combinations above right are listed by stocks with scions following. Those with an asterisk (*) make a weak union that may break or die after a time (possibly several years).

ALMOND: any almond; peach; nectarine

APPLE: any apple (but not vigorous and slow varieties together).

APRICOT: any apricot; peach*; plum; nectarine*

CHERRY, sour; any cherry, sweet or sour

CHERRY, sweet; any cherry

ORANGE: any orange; grapefruit; lemon

PEACH: any peach or nectarine; almond; apricot; plum

PEAR: any pear

PLUM, European: any European plum; almond; apricot; peach*; nectarine; Japanese plum

PLUM, Japanese: any Japanese plum; European plum*; apricot; peach*; nectarine

QUINCE: any quince (*Cydonia*); pear (not Bartlett)

Dwarfing rootstocks

Fruit varieties grafted onto certain rootstocks are dwarfed to a certain extent. Apples are usually dwarfed on the Malling and Malling-Merton series of rootstocks, each of which gives a mature tree of a different size. See the illustration on page 13 for comparative sizes of mature apple trees on these numbered roots.

Apricots are dwarfed to some extent when grafted onto the Western sand cherry, *Prunus besseyi*.

Sweet cherries are slightly dwarfed on roots of 'Stockton Morello' sour cherry.

Many citrus varieties are dwarfed on roots of the trifoliate orange.

Peaches are somewhat dwarfed on Nanking cherry roots.

Pears are dwarfed on quince roots, but since some varieties of pear will not form a union with quince, a double graft is often necessary, with quince at the root, a trunk section or interstock of Old Home or Hardy pear, and a top of the desired fruiting variety. Quince is an unsatisfactory rootstock in cold climates.

Plums are somewhat dwarfed on Western sand cherry roots.

Quince and sour cherry are not normally dwarfed by grafting.

Where to look for scionwood

An obvious source of scions for grafting is a neighbor's or friend's tree, but any nursery in bareroot season will have a large supply of scions, since the young trees must be cut back for planting. To obtain scions of old varieties, refer to sources in the "Old Apples" section beginning on page 28. Hold any scionwood in moist, cold surroundings until grafting season. A crisper in the refrigerator is a good place for scions. In cold climates, scions may be cut before the ground freezes and then bundled and buried below freezing level. The hole must be well drained and each variety should have a label so you won't confuse them.

Most scions should be cut in late fall or winter, but budsticks are also cut in spring and summer. See the pages on grafting methods for more detail.

T-budding

Use the budding method on stock branches from pencil size to 1 inch across. You have a choice of seasons: a. in spring at the first signs of stock growth (use dormant scions from storage); b. in May or early June when the new growth has mature leaves; c. in summer, from July through September, if bark is still loose on stock branches.

You can bud only when the bark of stock plants "slips," that is, when it detaches easily from the wood beneath. This happens during periods of active growth. Check the bark before beginning by making the T-shaped cut described below. If the bark sticks or breaks in spring, wait a while. If bark sticks in later summer, water thoroughly and wait a week.

Cut budsticks for early spring budding in winter and store them in a moist, cold place. Cut budsticks for May and June, or for summer just before you need them. Since they will have mature leaves you must cut these off, but leave the stems attached. They can serve as handles when you slice off individual buds. (The buds on new wood are just above the leaf stems.)

Use leaf buds and not flower buds in budding.

Normally, leaf buds are small, flat, and pointed, while flower buds are more rounded and protruding. If you are not sure, compare all the branches from which you intend cutting budsticks, and choose the smallest, flattest buds. If you find that you have made a mistake in early spring, you can try again in May or in summer.

Buds inserted in the spring months will grow during the same season. Check them three weeks after budding, and if they look healthy or show signs of expanding, cut the stock branch off above the next leaf or shoot. Cut this short piece when bud is well grown. Again, if you're not sure, wait a week or two. Buds inserted in summer will not grow until the following spring. Do not cut the stock away until growing season begins. You can be fairly sure that the bud will grow if the bit of stem you leave drops away, leaving a healthy-looking bud. If the stem shrivels without dropping and the bud turns black you have failed. Try again if the bark is still slipping.

Step 1
With a sharp knife, make a cut about 1½ inches long down the middle of a smooth stock branch. Cut through bark to wood. Cut across to form a T; pry up a corner. If bark is not loose, water and wait, or try again the following spring.

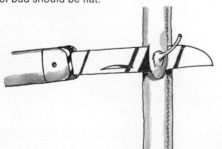

Step 2
Cut a pencil-sized branch or budstick. Snip leaves, if present, leaving stems. Cut off immature wood at branch tips. Avoid large, rounded buds. They may be flower buds.

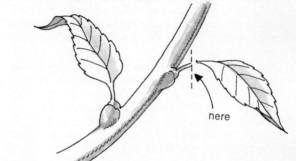

here

Step 3
With very sharp knife, slice upward from ¾ inch below bud to 1 inch above. Take a sliver of wood with the bud. Back of bud should be flat.

Step 4
Cut across the top of bud sliver (shield) about ¾ inch above the bud. Lift it off without touching raw cut. Use knife blade or stem segment to handle.

Step 5
Slide bud shield into T-cut, using point of knife below bud to push it down. Straight top of shield should match top of T-cut on stock. Wrap with a length of flat rubber band, winding end into first loop. Finish tie by inserting end in last turn.

Step 6
If bud joins to stock, remove rubber and cut stock in 6 to 8 weeks for early-season budding, or wait until following spring for summer budding.

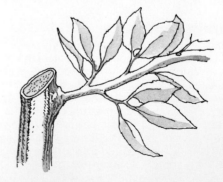

Whip graft

The whip graft is easy for a beginner, and can be used either to graft a desired variety to a young rootstock or to add varieties to upper branches of a young tree. Use it to join branches from ¼ to ½ inch in diameter.

Whip grafts should be made in very early spring, either at the earliest signs of stock growth, or just before growth begins. The bark need not slip. Scion wood can be cut in late fall and winter and stored, or cut when you graft.

The technique described below is the standard method, used for grafting branches, or for grafting a section of root to a scion for a new plant. There are variations that also work well if you are careful.

For topworking new varieties into a young tree, you can make only the sloping cut omitting the reverse cut in drawing 3 below.

For grafting a small scion to a larger stock, you can match the cambium on one side of the stock only, leaving part of the cut on the stock uncovered.

Do not graft a large scion to a smaller stock. It is likely to dry out and die and, if it grows, the callus tissue will be excessive, forming a large knot at the joint.

Scions should be 2 or 3 buds long for whip grafting, but if a longer piece is easier to handle, clip it once the graft is tied, then wax the end cut.

You will know that the graft is successful if the scion grows.

Plastic stretch tape may be left in place through the first growing season. Ties that will not stretch must be carefully cut once growth is well started. It is a good idea to apply a tree seal or pruning paint to the graft area after tape is removed. This gives protection from the sun and other elements.

Step 1
Compare scion and stock. Scion should be of same diameter as stock or somewhat smaller. Find a section of each that is free of buds.

Step 2
With a very sharp knife, make a smooth, sloping cut on stock and scion from 1 to 2½ inches long. A wavy cut will join poorly or fail to join.

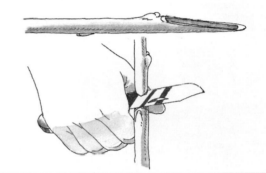

Step 3
Make reverse cuts on both scion and stock, beginning about a third of the way from tip. (It is possible to skip this step if you join cambium carefully.)

Step 4
Slide scion and stock together so that cambium is carefully matched on at least one side of stock. Stock can be slightly wider than scion.

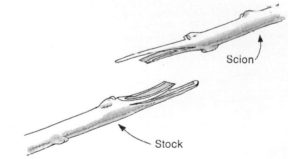

Step 5
Bind with plastic stretch tape or with budding rubbers or raffia. Cover entire length of cut and wax. Snip all but 3 buds.

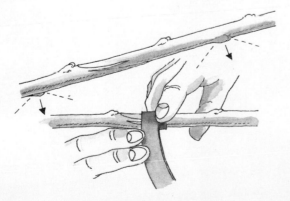

Step 6
When growth begins, cut nonstretch ties such as raffia. Stretch tape may be left until following season.

Elec. tape

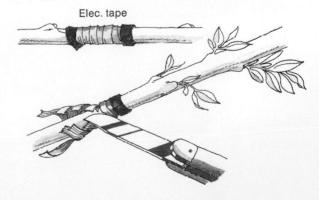

Cleft graft

Cleft grafts can be made on stocks from 1 to 4 inches in diameter. The scions used are much smaller, approximately pencil-sized. The season for cleft grafting is very early spring when buds first begin to swell, although it is possible to graft during winter if it is more convenient. The bark should not yet be slipping or it may come loose when the stock is split.

The season for cleft grafting will vary, depending on the kind of tree to be grafted. Almonds or apricots begin growth and bloom earlier than apples or pears, so the proper season may extend from January to March or later in cold climates.

Scions can be cut and stored, or cut when you graft. Since the scions will be much smaller than the stock, be especially careful to match the cambium layer. If bark is thick on the stock, then the scions when properly matched will sit well in from the stock surface.

Two or three scion buds should protrude from the stock, but you can work with a longer scion, then snip and wax it once grafts are in place.

In cleft grafting, waxing is especially important. Wax thickly after matching scions and stock, then check every few days and rewax any splits. Use grafting wax or water-base asphalt tree seal applied with a flat stick. Never use sprays to coat grafting wounds as they are not thick enough. If you think that sunny weather may follow your grafting, paint stock and scion with an interior latex paint to prevent sunburn.

Don't worry if wax covers the scion buds. They easily push through when they begin to grow.

For very small branches where the cleft does not hold the scions firmly, wrap the stock with plastic tape for more security.

Step 1
Find a branch 1 to 4 inches in diameter with a very straight smooth portion. Saw the branch straight across, leaving this smooth area for splitting. Use a heavy knife, cleaver, or special tool for splitting, placing it across the center of the cut and tapping with a mallet. Split 2 to 3 inches down.

Step 2
Push a large screwdriver or chisel into the center of the split to hold it open for the scions.

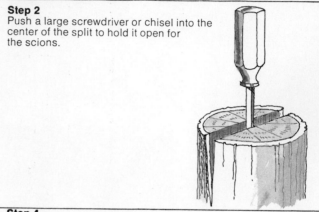

Step 3
Use two scions. Cut into a wedge shape with the angle of the cut made to match the opening in the stock. Insert scions with cambium touching cambium of stock along length of wedge cut. Remove screwdriver to pinch scions in cleft.

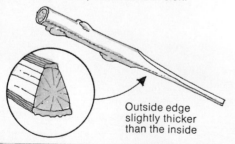

Outside edge slightly thicker than the inside

Step 4
End view of scion in stock should look like this. Side view of scion should look like this.

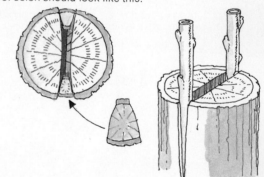

Step 5
Wax stock, filling cleft, and coat scions heavily along sides. Clip to 3 buds if necessary and wax end cut. Paint with white interior latex in sunny weather.

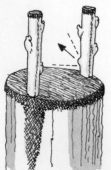

Step 6
If only one scion grows, cut stock at an angle and paint with pruning compound. If both grow, head back the weaker, but leave it to help heal stock.

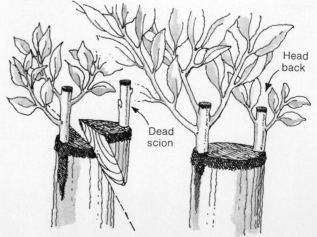

Head back

Dead scion

Bark grafting

Bark grafts can be performed on stock branches from 1 inch to 12 or more inches in diameter, but very large stocks are less satisfactory since the cut heals slowly or not at all. Optimum size of stock is from two to five inches in diameter.

The season for bark grafting is later than for either the whip or cleft method, since the bark must "slip" or detach easily. Check for slipping on a small branch before making a major cut.

Scions must be cut early and held in a cold place, since otherwise they will not be fully dormant at the season when bark is slipping. Insert several scions of the same kind around the stock, and allow the strongest to grow. Head the others back, but keep

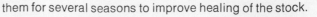

them for several seasons to improve healing of the stock.

The method described here is one of several, each differing in the way the stock bark is cut and the scion trimmed. This method offers double cambium contact of scion and stock and the simple trimming of the scion is easy for a beginner. Cooperative Extension pamphlets are available describing other methods. Again, thorough waxing is most important. Check frequently for splits and rewax if necessary.

You can use bark grafting to replace an entire tree if it is not too large. Cut off the top, leaving one foot of smooth-barked trunk, then graft on your scions. This method will only work on deciduous material. To replace the top of an evergreen, you must leave a "nurse" branch of the original tree until the scions are well grown.

Step 1
First choose 3 or 4 scions of about pencil size and snip them to about 6 inches long. Then find a smooth, straight section on the stock and saw it straight across. See pruning section for proper three-step cut to prevent torn bark.

Step 2
Hold a single scion against the bark of the stock and nick the stock on each side of it. Then cut downward through the bark of the stock 1 or 2 inches and peel back the flap.

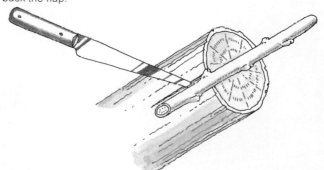

Step 3
Slice the base of the scion at an angle to form a sloping cut as long as the flap of bark on the stock. On the other side of the scion, make another sloping cut about ⅓ as long.

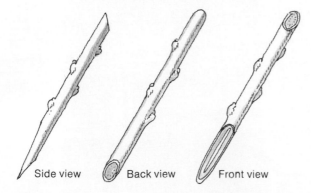

Side view   Back view   Front view

Step 4
Place the long cut flat against the wood of the stock. Nail it with a small nail near the top of the stock. Press the bark flap against the scion and nail it below the first nail. You can cut any section of flap beyond the short cut on the scion. Repeat steps 2, 3, and 4 for each scion up to 4.

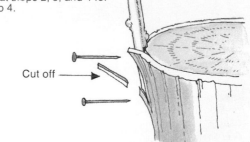

Cut off →

Step 5
When all scions are tacked in place, wax heavily to cover all joints. Snip scions to 2 or 3 buds and wax end cut.

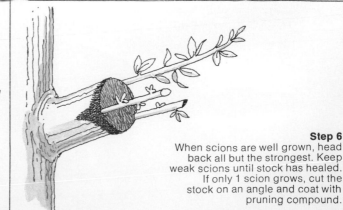

Step 6
When scions are well grown, head back all but the strongest. Keep weak scions until stock has healed. If only 1 scion grows, cut the stock on an angle and coat with pruning compound.

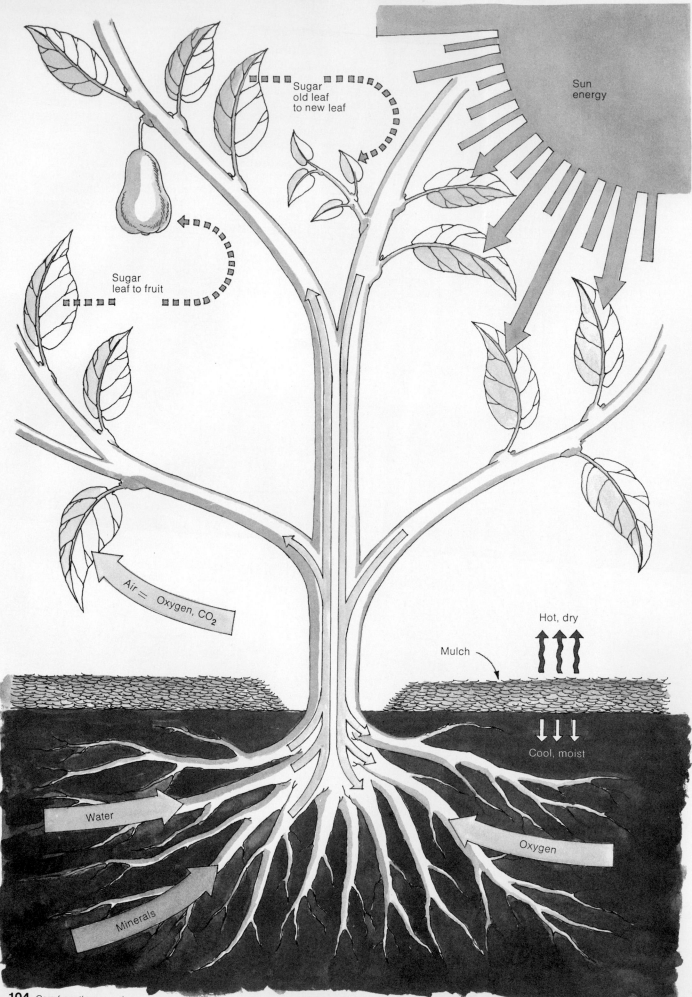

Care from the ground up

When the roots are happy, the plant is healthy. Here's how to plant, feed, water, and mulch to keep things growing smoothly under the garden floor.

The fruiting plants discussed in this book have been selected over the centuries because they produce much finer crops than their wild relatives. The extra crop, though, means that there's more stress on the plant . . . it has, so to speak, more mouths to feed. You have to help by providing an ideal environment.

The illustration on the opposite page will give you an idea of the day-to-day work of a fruit plant.

Sweetness and light

All plants need a lot of sugar. They make it themselves in their leaves, using carbon dioxide, water, and the energy of sunlight. You help out by planting in a sunny spot, pruning and training for good leaf exposure, keeping water in the soil, and keeping leaves free of dust, pests, and disease so that they can do their work. Each growing piece of fruit needs some 30 leaves working for it, not to speak of leaves supplying nourishment to the roots and branches.

Here's what you buy

The first step in producing fruit is buying a plant. Most deciduous fruit plants are sold bareroot. The leafless plant is pulled out of the ground in late fall or winter and shipped to the nursery where it is held in moist sand or wood shavings. Sometimes each root is enclosed in a plastic bag full of moist shavings. A bareroot plant is fragile and must be kept cool and moist. Plant it as soon as possible after you get it, instructions follow on page 108.

Evergreen plants are sold with their roots wrapped in soil and burlap, or they are growing in metal or pulp containers. The burlapped form is sold at the same season as bareroot plants and should go into the ground quickly. The container form may be sold at any time and you can wait a while to plant if you don't cut the container.

Bareroot plants are sometimes put into containers at the nursery. If you buy them in winter, or while they're still dormant, you can bare the roots again to plant them. If they have leafed out, grow them in their containers until May or June, so the root system has time to knit the container soil together.

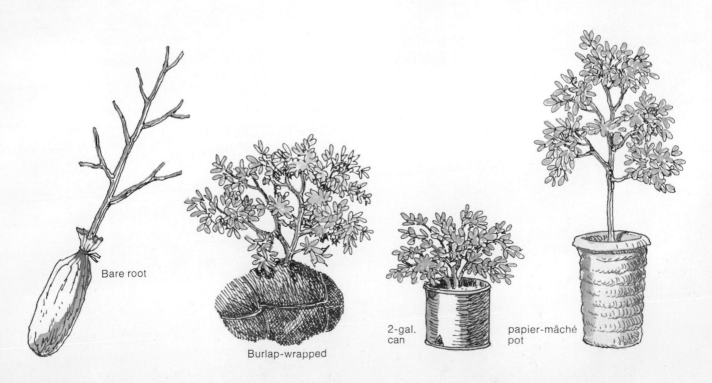

Bare root

Burlap-wrapped

2-gal. can

papier-mâché pot

Deep-down goodness

While the leaves are busy topside, the roots spread out underground, searching for water and minerals. They won't spread very fast or far in dense, wet soil with no air spaces, since they need a good supply of oxygen. You help to supply it by adding organic material, such as compost, to densely packed clay soils.

Roots grow only where there's the right amount of moisture, and you help here too by watering deeply and regularly, and covering the surface with a mulch to keep things cool and damp.

Apart from moisture, the roots are looking primarily for minerals. The one that's always in short supply is a usable form of nitrogen. You have to add it several times from early spring into summer. Sometimes your soil will turn out to be short of some other mineral. Your Cooperative Extension Agent can tell you whether you should add such things as potassium, iron, or zinc, and how to do it. Don't worry about these things unless your tree starts to look strange. It may turn yellow or red, drop leaves out of season, or produce an odd-looking crop. Describe symptoms or show an odd branch and the Extension Office can take it from there.

The enemy

Since you like fruit, it's no surprise that many other creatures do too, from birds and mice, to insects, to fungi and bacteria. Part of the battle is keeping the plant clean and growing. Supply what it needs and hose it down if it's dusty. Sprays won't do their job if a plant is filthy and starving.

Common pests and diseases appear on pages 74 to 77. Most of them have done their damage once you notice them, so you spray ahead of time. For example, codling moths lay eggs in flowers. You spray when petals have fallen. It's no good spraying when you see wormholes and misshapen fruit.

Your soil—what's it like?

Here's what plants need down where the roots grow:

1. Air in the soil
2. Constant moisture (but not standing water)
3. A supply of mineral nutrients

You'll supply these needs best if you examine your soil. Is it rock-hard when dry, and gummy when wet? Then you probably have the very fine soil called clay or adobe. It holds moisture so well that there's often no room for air. Fluff it up with organic material like compost or peat moss. Spread four or five inches of organic matter over the soil and stir it in, mixing evenly. Ideally, you should add the material wherever the plant's roots might spread when it's mature, and they'll spread more widely than the branches.

Does water sink right in without spreading much? Does the soil dry up just a few days after watering? Sandy

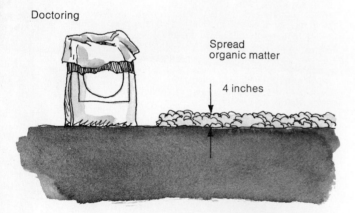

Doctoring

Spread organic matter

4 inches

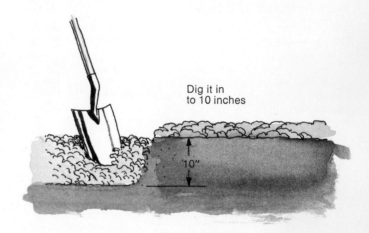

Dig it in to 10 inches

10"

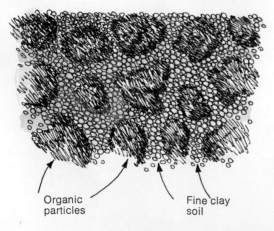

Clay is fluffier

Organic particles

Fine clay soil

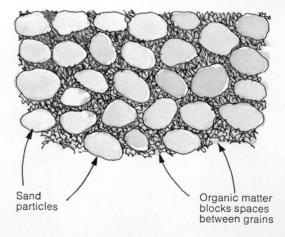

Sand holds water

Sand particles

Organic matter blocks spaces between grains

soils are like this. They have lots of air, but moisture and nutrients disappear fast. Organic matter helps here too, by filling in spaces between the coarse soil particles and holding onto the water you deliver. Peat moss, compost, and manures are especially good materials for sandy soil. Sawdust and ground bark are less good at water holding and poor at hanging on to nutrients.

If you have soil that feels moist for days after watering, but still crumbles easily when you pick up a handful and squeeze it, then its just right.

Keeping soil healthy

Once a planting area is in good shape and your plant is in the ground, keep it growing by protecting the soil. Sun and wind will cause bare soil to crust over at the surface. Then, air and water can't penetrate evenly and roots near the crust die out. Cover the soil surface as suggested under Mulch on page 110.

Foot traffic beats down the soil until air is driven out and water won't penetrate. A mulch helps here too, since it makes a cushion of resilient material over the root area.

Plants aren't all the same

Some plants tolerate dense, airless, soggy soil better than others. This list may help you decide what to plant, but keep in mind that in gardens with extremely dense soil you can still plant air-lovers in a raised bed one to three feet deep and wide enough to accommodate a good root system, perhaps six feet by six feet for a standard tree.

Tolerate dense or wet soil: pear, quince, cranberry

Tolerate short airless periods: apple, crabapple

Need fair drainage: apricot, cherry, fig, nectarine, peach, plum, grape, currant

Need good drainage: strawberry, cane berries, citrus

Need perfect drainage: blueberry

In a container

Think of a container as any limited area of good soil, and you'll see that it can be more than just a pot. If you dig a large hole in extremely poor clay soil and add a lot of organic material, the plant you put in the hole may never send roots beyond its borders. You have planted in a container within the soil. If you lift a plant above the soil in a raised bed, you create a kind of container. And of course if you plant in a pot or box on your deck or paving, you are planting in a container.

Container soil must be especially good, since the roots of the plant within it can't grow outward in search of a better life. It should drain very quickly, but hold moisture and nutrients. Normally a fruit plant will need a large volume of container soil, and it is cheaper to mix it yourself than to buy ready-mixed kinds.

Synthetic soils

The mixes, such as Jiffy-Mix and Redi-Earth, are referred to as "soilless mixes" or "synthetic soils." However you should not translate the word synthetic as *artificial*. The ingredients are as natural as Mother Nature could make them.

Jiffy-Mix, the most widely available synthetic soil, is made up of 50% peat moss and 50% vermiculite. When mined, vermiculite (Terralite) resembles mica. Under heat treatment the mineral flakes expand with air spaces to 20 times their original thickness.

Jiffy-Mix contains just enough nutrients to sustain initial plant growth. Use it to germinate seeds and for growing flower and vegetable transplants.

It provides what a plant needs for optimum growth:

1) Fast drainage of water through the "soil."

2) Good aeration—a high percentage of air in the "soil" after drainage.

3) A reservoir of water in the soil after drainage.

Air and water retention. The airspace after drainage and the water retention properties of various mixes and the materials that go into them has been measured. The figures shown in the chart below indicate percent by volume. Physical properties of clay loam are included in the list for comparison.

Material	Total Porosity	Water Retention	Air Space After Drainage
Clay loam	59.6	54.9	4.7
Sphagnum peat moss	84.2	58.8	25.4
Fine sand	44.6	38.7	5.9
Redwood sawdust	77.2	49.3	27.9
Perlite, 1/16-3/16"	77.1	47.3	29.8
Vermiculite, 0-3/16"	80.5	53.0	27.5
Fir bark, 0-1/8"	69.5	38.0	31.5
1:1, fine sand: fir bark	54.6	37.4	15.2
1:1, fine sand: peat moss	56.7	47.3	9.4
1:1, perlite, peat moss	74.9	51.3	23.6

The synthetic mix is free of disease organisms, insects and weed seeds. It eliminates disease problems often present in regular soil.

It is light weight—half the weight of soil when both are wet. The light weight is an advantage when growing plants in containers on roofs or balconies.

You can use the mix just as it comes from the bag. But thorough wetting before use is absolutely necessary. And "thorough wetting" is not easy with dry peat moss. We wet it by putting the amount we want to use in a plastic bag, adding *warm* water, and then squeezing and mixing the bag by hand.

One 4-cubic foot bag will fill a planter box 24 by 36 inches, by 8 inches deep.

Many gardeners add top soil to the mix when planting shrubs and trees in containers. This gives them a soil of good physical properties, but all the advantages of sterilization are lost.

We make our own mix when planting a number of trees and shrubs, or when filling a raised bed. The properties for a mix to be used in landscape plantings might be:

9 cubic feet of fine sand
18 cubic feet of ground bark or
nitrogen-stabilized sawdust
or
9 cubic feet of fine sand
9 cubic feet of peat moss
9 cubic feet of ground bark
add to either of the above:
5 pounds of 5-10-10 fertilizer
7 pounds of ground limestone
1 pound of iron sulphate

Planting

The illustrations here will give you an idea how to plant a tree from the nursery. Here are some special points to remember:

✔Never plant if the soil is very wet. Working wet soil packs it and traps roots. In very rainy climates, you can dig holes for bareroot and burlap-wrapped plants in fall and protect the soil removed from the hole with a weighted plastic sheet. It will be workable any time.

✔Never let bareroot or burlap-wrapped plants lie around unprotected. If you must bring bareroot plants home before youn can plant, dig a shallow trench, lay the plants on their sides with roots in the trench, and cover roots with moist soil. Wrap burlapped plants in a sheet of plastic so the soil ball stays moist.

✔Plant high. Notice in the illustrations that the planting soil is mounded above the normal soil line. The most fragile part of a woody plant is the crown, that section where soil touches the trunk and the roots branch. It must be dry most of the time and especially in spring and fall. Raised planting minimizes crown rot (which could be fatal to the plant) by making it impossible for water to puddle near the trunk. If you plant at soil level, you're inviting disaster because the soil in the planting hole will settle and your plants will sink downward.

Fertilizing

When you feed a fruit tree, you are supplementing the mineral elements in the soil. Nitrogen is the element most commonly in short supply so it becomes the key nutrient in a fertilizer program. Most fruit tree fertilizers will contain higher amounts of nitrogen than other nutrients, for example, 12-6-6 or 12-6-10. Straight nitrogen forms are ammonium nitrate, calcium nitrate, urea, and ammonium sulfate. The choice of nutrients to use depends upon several factors.

Since fruit trees are grown in so many different types of soils, it is virtually impossible to pin down the specific fertilizer needs. Also, there are many selections and

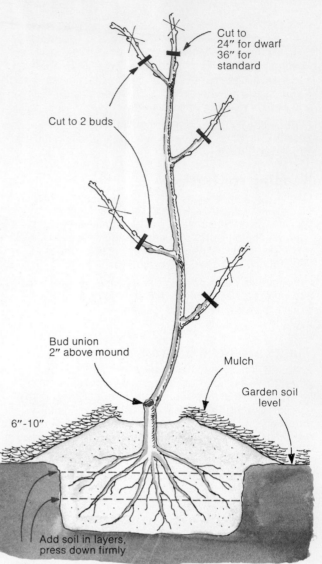

Cut to 24" for dwarf 36" for standard

Cut to 2 buds

Bud union 2" above mound

Mulch

Garden soil level

6"-10"

Add soil in layers, press down firmly

Bareroot tree

Clip off broken roots, leaving clean cut. Rub off fine root hairs. Hole must be wide enough for roots to spread. Soak soil after hole is refilled, make volcano-shaped mound, soak again from top, running water slowly so it sinks in. Mound higher in dense soil, lower in good soil.

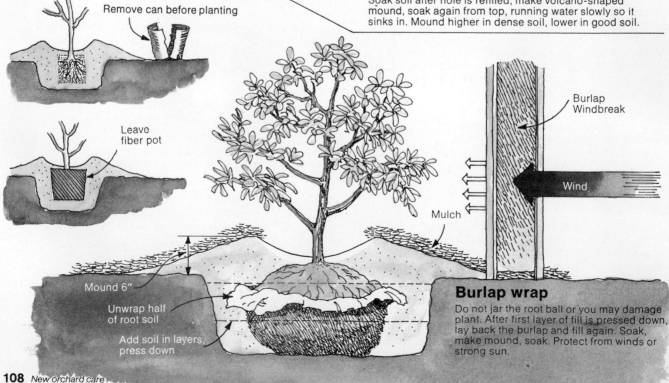

Remove can before planting

Leave fiber pot

Burlap Windbreak

Wind

Mulch

Mound 6"

Unwrap half of root soil

Add soil in layers, press down

Burlap wrap

Do not jar the root ball or you may damage plant. After first layer of fill is pressed down, lay back the burlap and fill again. Soak, make mound, soak. Protect from winds or strong sun.

varieties that respond differently. The trees themselves can often serve as indicators of needs. If growth is vigorous and healthy and leaves appear normal, then nutrient requirements are being met. But, if growth is limited and the leaves are small or pale green or chlorotic, fertilizer is needed.

It's not a good practice to let your trees demonstrate these needs; preventing these deficiency signals is a much better practice.

When to feed . . . how much

We suggest applying one-half of the fertilizer in the spring, and the other half after harvest for early-bearing trees or about mid-June for later-bearing varieties. Keep the fertilizer at least a foot away from the trunk and apply evenly under the tree canopy.

A general rule of thumb is to use about ¾ lb. of nitrogen for each mature tree (not dwarf varieties) per year. This means that for fertilizer having 12% nitrogen you will need to apply 6 pounds. Young trees will need correspondingly lesser amounts and newly planted trees should not be fertilized with nitrogen until the root system becomes well established. Follow label directions on the fertilizer package.

Potassium and other nutrients. Potassium is commonly deficient in fruit trees, particularly in high rainfall areas and where trees are grown on sandy or gravelly soils. Be sure to include potassium in the fertilizer program where these conditions exist. Manures contain potash so this nutrient is added when manures are used.

Phosphorous fertilizers should be added to the planting hole and mixed with the soil since phosphorus is very important when the root system is limited. If after following the usual fertilizer program, growth is still weak and leaves show abnormal appearances, then zinc, magnesium, iron, manganese, and boron could be deficient. A foliar spray during the growing season may be the best way of applying these elements.

Feeding with animal manure. Animal manures are suitable as fertilizers but use them with caution since they often contain harmful amounts of salts and obnoxious weed seeds. Also remember that bird and rabbit manures contain from 3-6 times more nitrogen than cattle or horse manure, so use lesser amounts. About 30-60 pounds of bird or rabbit manure and 100-200 pounds of cattle manure per tree will supply the nutrient needs of full size mature trees. Spread it under the branches in the fall or early spring. For young trees use about ⅓ pound of bird or rabbit manure, or one pound of cattle manure per tree each year. Double the amount each year to maturity.

Judging the results. Using the appearance of the tree as a fertilization guide is a good practice if you don't let them get overly deficient. Use sufficient fertilizer each year to keep the trees growing well — excess growth means to cut back — deficient growth means to use more. Follow the label directions of reputable fertilizer companies and the advice of your informed nurseryman.

Dwarf and container plantings

Since these never grow very big, they require lesser amounts of fertilizers. Start out with ¼ cup of a 12-6-6 grade fertilizer (or similar analysis) after the tree is well established. Repeat this application annually, supplementing it with small additions (⅛ cup increments) every two to three months during the growing season until the tree seems to be doing well. Adjust if growth is too slow or too vigorous.

Watering

A standard fruit tree needs deep watering. Dwarf trees on shallow-rooted stocks may not need as much but any tree must have a constant moisture supply. Here's how to provide it.

At planting time. Water each layer of soil in the planting hole. If the garden soil is dry, soak the hole itself before you put in the plant. Finish by soaking from the top of the planting mound, creating a volcano-like depression to hold the water. Let the hose trickle so water won't run over the side.

After planting, and before growth begins, don't water again unless the soil seems unusually dry. The roots are not in active growth, and soggy soil will rot them.

When growth begins, give the plants a soaking when the top inch or so of soil dries. Dig down to be sure water is needed. Water with a trickling hose at the top of the planting mound. This is especially important with burlap-wrapped plants, since the soil in the ball may not take up water unless you trickle it straight into the ball.

When first-season growth is abundant. In midsummer, when plants are growing well, stop watering from the top of the mound. Create a shallow ditch right at the base of the planting mound and soak the soil in this circular ditch about every two to three weeks, or when the top inch or two dries.

Watering after the first season. Make a shallow ditch about 6 to 12 inches wide around the plant and just outside the tips of the branches. Move the ditch outward as the plant grows. Soak thoroughly about once every three to four weeks. This is a rough guide. Your tree may need water every two weeks in very sandy soil, or not for six weeks in heavy soil. Dig down to check the moisture in the upper few inches before watering. Conserve the water you provide by spreading a 2-inch layer of mulch over the roots from the mound area to the outside of the watering ditch.

How long to water. You want to soak the soil long enough to force water down to the deep roots. On dwarf trees the deepest roots may stop 30 to 36 inches below the surface. On big trees, the roots may extend many feet. Then too, water sinks quickly through sandy soil, but very slowly through clay. A day after keeping your watering ditch full for two or three hours, check penetration by pushing a 4- or 5-foot length of stiff wire into the wet soil. It will penetrate only wet soil, so when it refuses to go down any farther, pull it out and check the depth of penetration. Soil should be moist down to at least 2½ feet for dwarfs, 3½ to 4 for big trees.

Trees in a lawn area should have a deep soak about twice a summer, in addition to lawn watering.

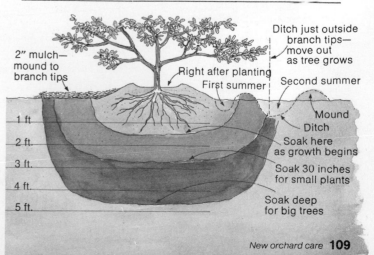

2" mulch—mound to branch tips

Ditch just outside branch tips—move out as tree grows

Right after planting / First summer

Second summer

Mound

Ditch

Soak here as growth begins

Soak 30 inches for small plants

Soak deep for big trees

1 ft.
2 ft.
3 ft.
4 ft.
5 ft.

Mulch the root zone

Mulch is just a cover over the soil. It might be gravel, plastic, ground fir bark, manure—or even grass clippings, leaves, or brown paper bags. It is important for many reasons.

✔ Mulch keeps wind and sun from baking and crusting soil.

✔ Mulch smothers weed seeds.

✔ Mulch protects soil from foot traffic.

✔ Mulch holds in water even at the surface.

✔ Mulch keeps surface soil cool.

✔ Mulch keeps soil from freezing and thawing, which causes heaving of plants.

✔ Organic mulches rot, improve soil texture.

When and where to mulch

Cover the soil with a mulch from the planting mound to the branch tips if you can. Use at least two inches of a porous material like manure. Slash waterproof mulches like thick paper or plastic so water can pass through. Beautify a plastic mulch with gravel, pebbles, or bark chips spread over the surface about an inch deep. To hide paper mulches cover them with a thin layer of ground bark.

In warm, dry climates, spread mulch in spring and then turn it into the top two inches of soil in late fall. In cold climates where ground may freeze, add more mulch in late fall, up to six inches. You may even want to cover this deep mulch with evergreen boughs for added protection from freezing, and to keep the mulch in place when strong winds blow. Snow adds to the usefulness of any mulch.

Never pile any mulch against the tree trunk or plant stem. Keep it at least six inches away. Wet mulch there can cause rot, and dwarf trees mulched to the bud union will take root and grow to full size. An exception: in very cold climates, mulch deeply over the bud union when real cold begins, remove the mulch when severe cold is over.

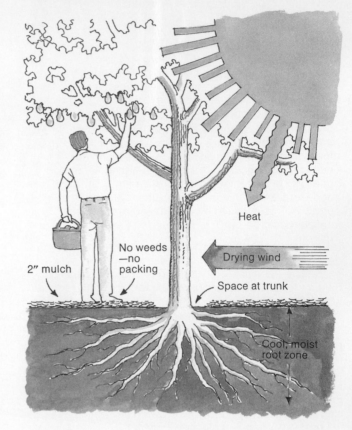

Heat

2″ mulch

No weeds —no packing

Drying wind

Space at trunk

Cool, moist root zone

Mulching materials

Material	Remarks
Rotted manure	May contain weed seeds.
Sawdust Wood chips Wood shavings	Low in plant nutrients, decomposes slowly, tends to pack down. Well-rotted material preferred. Can be fresh if nitrate of ammonia or nitrate of soda is added at the rate of 1 pound per 100 sq. ft. Keep away from building foundations; may cause termites.
Peat moss	Attractive, available, but expensive for large areas. Should be kept moist at all times.
Ground corn cobs	Excellent for improving soil structure.
Pine needles	Will not mat down. Fairly durable.
Peanut hulls Cotton screenings Tobacco stems (shredded)	Supply plant nutrients and improve soil structure. Fairly durable.
Tree leaves (whole) Tree leaves (shredded)	Excellent source of humus. Rot rapidly, high in nutrients. Oak leaves especially valuable for azaleas, camellias, and rhododendrons.
Hay Grass clippings	Unattractive, but repeated use builds up reserve of available nutrients which lasts for years.
Straw	Same as above, but lower in nutrients although furnishes considerable potassium.
Buckwheat hulls	Very attractive but tend to scatter in windy locations.
Pecan hulls	Extremely durable, availability limited.
Gravel or stone chips	Limited use, but particularly good for rock garden plantings. Extremely durable, holds down weeds, but does not supply plant nutrients or humus.
Bark	Ground and packaged commercially. Especially attractive in this form. Sometimes available in rough form from pulpwood-loading sites.

List of catalog sources

Throughout the book, we give a list of source numbers after each variety name. You will notice an "s" or "D" after some numbers. This means that semi-dwarf or dwarf plants are available.

The numbers in the varieties lists are the same as those shown below. They show which firms to write to for catalogs.

In our listing of available catalogs we have given a brief description of each source. By reading those descriptions you can determine the companies that are specialists in fruits and those that cover the entire spectrum of garden material.

Many of these catalogs are the equivalents of garden books containing good reference material. They reward the careful reader.

Our catalog search was made with 1976 information. You can expect changes in the catalogs of later dates. What is scarce today may be widely available in future years, but our search will uncover the most likely sources of hard-to-find varieties.

Look at the source listings to see if they are wholesale or retail dealers. Wholesale cannot sell directly to you, but you can refer your nurseryman to them.

1. Adams County Nursery & Fruit Farms
   Aspers, PA 17304
   Fruit specialists. 22-page catalog.
   Wholesale and retail

2. Bountiful Ridge Nurseries, Inc.
   Box 250
   Princess Anne, MD 21853
   Specialists in fruits and nuts.
   50-page catalog and planting guide.
   Wholesale and retail.

3. Bowers Berry Nursery
   94959 Hwy 99 E
   Junction City, OR 97448
   12-page catalog of berries and grapes. Wholesale and retail.

4. Bunting's Berries
   Selbyville, DE 19975
   40-page catalog. 24 pages strawberries. Fruit trees, berries, and nursery stock.

5. Burgess Seed and Plant Co.
   P.O. Box 82
   Galesburg, MI 49053
   Two catalogs are offered:
   1. 44-page general seed catalog. Flowers, vegetables, and nursery stock. 4 pages on fruit.
   2. Especially for the limited space gardener. Full color, 32-page catalog with one page on fruits to grow indoors.

6. W. Atlee Burpee Co.
   Warminster, PA 18974
   Clinton, IA 52732
   Riverside, CA 92502
   180-page general seed catalog. Flowers, vegetables, garden aids, and nursery stock. 10 pages on fruit.

7. C & O Nursery
   P.O. Box 116
   1700 N. Wenatchee Ave.
   Wenatchee, WA 98801
   Fruit specialists. Exclusive patented varieties. 40-page catalog with 7 pages of ornamentals and shade trees. Wholesale and retail.

8. The Clyde Nursery
   On Highway U.S. 20
   Clyde, OH 43410
   10-page catalog of fruits and berries.

9. Columbia Basin Nursery
   Box 458
   Quincy, WA 98848
   Colored brochure and price list. Seedling rootstock, dwarfing apple rootstock, dwarf and standard budded fruit trees. Wholesale and retail.

10. L. E. Cooke Co.
    26333 Road 140
    Visalia, CA 93277
    Fruits, berries, grapes, vegetables, and nursery stock. Specializes in dwarf and semidwarf fruit trees and genetic dwarf peaches. Wholesale only. Inquiries answered with information on retail availability.

11. Cumberland Valley Nurseries, Inc.
    P.O. Box 430
    113 Lind Street
    McMinnville, TN 37110
    1-page catalog specializing in plums, peaches, and nectarines. Wholesale and retail.

12. Farmer Seed & Nursery Co.
    Faribault, MN 55021
    84-page general seed catalog. Flowers, vegetables, and nursery stock. 5 pages on fruit.

13. Henry Field Seed & Nursery Co.
    407 Sycamore Street
    Shenandoah, IA 51601
    116-page general seed and nursery catalog. Flowers, vegetables, gardening aids, and nursery stock. 16 pages on fruit.

14. Dean Foster Nurseries
    Hartford, MI 49257
    80-page general catalog. Specializing in strawberries. Flowers, vegetables, dwarf fruit, and berries. Wholesale and retail.

15. Fowler Nurseries, Inc.
    525 Fowler Road
    Newcastle, CA 95658
    4-page price list of over 200 varieties sent on request. Commercial price list also available. 32-page catalog $1.

16. Grootendorst Nurseries
    Lakeside, MI 49116
    Specialists in dwarf Malling and Merton rootstock.

17. Gurney Seed & Nursery Co.
    1448 Page St.
    Yankton, SD 57078
    76-page general seed catalog. Flowers, vegetables, and nursery stock. 10 pages on fruit.

18. Haley Nursery Co., Inc.
    Smithville, TN 37116
    6-page price list. Fruit trees. Specializing in peaches and nectarines. Wholesale only. Ask your dealer to order.

19. Heath's Nursery, Inc.
    P.O. Box 707
    Brewster, WA 98812
    12-page catalog of fruit trees, shade and ornamental trees.

20. Inter-State Nurseries
    Hamburg, IA 51644
    84-page catalog. Fruit, flowers, berries, roses, and ornamentals. 14 pages on fruit.

21. Ison's Nursery & Vineyard
    Brooks, GA 30205
    16-page catalog specializing in grapes. Wholesale and retail.

22. J. W. Jung Seed Co.
Station 8
Randolph, WI 53956
60-page general seed catalog.
Flowers, vegetables, and nursery
stock, 4 pages on fruit.

23. Kelly Bros. Nurseries, Inc.
Dansville, NY 14437
80-page catalog of fruit, nuts,
flowers, and ornamentals.
16 pages on fruit.

24. Lawson's Nursery
Route 1, Box 61
Ball Ground, GA 30107
8-page fruit catalog.
Specializing in old-fashioned
and unusual fruit trees. Lists over
100 varieties of old apples.

25. Henry Leuthardt Nurseries, Inc.
East Moriches, Long Island, NY 11940
52-page fruit catalog and guidebook
on dwarf and espalier-trained fruit
trees.

26. Earl May Seed & Nursery Co.
Shenandoah, IA 51603
80-page general seed catalog.
Flowers, vegetables, and nursery
stock. 10 pages on fruit.

27. Miller's Nursery, Inc.
Canandaigua, NY 14424
Fruit specialists. 40-page catalog
also includes garden aids and
ornamentals.

28. New York State Fruit Testing
Cooperative Association
Geneva, NY 14456
32-page fruit catalog. $4 member-
ship fee, refunded on first order.

29. L. L. Olds Seed Co.
2901 Packers Ave.
Box 1069
Madison, WI 53701
80-page general seed catalog.
Flowers, vegetables, and nursery
stock. 3 pages on fruit.

30. Owen's Vineyard and Nursery
Georgia Highway 85
Gay, GA 30218
12-page catalog specializing
in muscadine grapes. Includes guidelines for growing and training. Southern rabbiteye blueberries available.

31. Rayner's Bros., Inc.
Salisbury, MD 21801

34-page fruit catalog specializing
in strawberries. 3 pages on fruit trees.

32. Southmeadow Fruit Gardens
2363 Tilbury Place
Birmingham, MI 48009
Probably the largest collection of
fruit varieties, old, new, and rare,
in the U.S. Their 112-page illustrated
catalog is priced at $5 and worth it.
A condensed 8-page catalog is free.

33. Stanek's Garden Center
East 2929 - 27th Avenue
Spokane, WA 99203
34-page catalog of fruit, flowers, and
ornamentals. 4 pages of fruit and
berries.

34. Stark Bros. Nursery
Louisiana, MO 73353
40-page illustrated catalog and
guide. 12 pages vegetables,
ornamentals, and nuts.

35. Van Well Nursery
P.O. Box 1339
Wenatchee, WA 98801
28-page fruit catalog. Fruits
and berries. Wholesale and retail.

36. Waynesboro Nurseries
P.O. Box 987
Waynesboro, VA 22980
48-page catalog on fruits, nuts and
ornamental plant material. 21 pages
on fruits and nuts.

37. Weeks Berry Nursery
6494 Windsor Island Rd. No.
Salem, OR 97303
Specialists in small fruits.
Wholesale and commercial plantings.

38. Dave Wilson Nursery
4306 Santa Fe Avenue
Hughson, CA 95326
Fruits, berries, grapes. Specializing
in Zaiger patented fruit trees. Wholesale only. Ask your dealer to order.

39. H. G. Hastings Co.
Box 4655
Atlanta, GA 30302
64-page general seed catalog.
Flowers, vegetables, and nursery
stock. 5 pages on fruits and berries.

40. Archias Seed Store Corp.
P.O. Box 109
Sedalia, MO 65301

42-page general seed catalog.
Flowers, vegetables, and nursery
stock. 4 pages on fruits and berries.

41. Whatley Nursery
Route 1, Box 197
Helena, GA 31037
2-page price list. Specializing in
muscadine grapes. Wholesale and
retail.

42. Buckley Nursery Co.
Rt. 2, Box 199
Buckley, WA 98321
44-page catalog. Fruit, shade,
flowers, and ornamental trees. 13
pages devoted to fruit. Wholesale
and retail.

43. C. D. Schwartze Nursery
2302 Tacoma Rd.
Puyallup, WA 98731
5-page catalog specializing in
apple trees and crab apple trees.

44. Hilltop Orchards & Nurseries, Inc.
Rt. 2
Hartford, MI 49057
Widely recognized fruit tree special-
ists for commercial orchardists.
Free, 38-page handbook and catalog.

45. Stribling Nurseries
1620 W. 16th—P.O. Box 793
Merced, CA 95340
Fruit specialists. 44-page catalog of
fruit, nut, and grape varieties.
Includes tree-planting guides and
ripening charts.

46. Armstrong Nurseries
P.O. Box 473
Ontario, CA 91761
Specialists in fruit trees and roses.
40-page catalog lists genetic dwarf
peaches and nectarines, as well as
other exotic fruit trees. Vegetables
and bulbs.

47. W. F. Allen Co.
P.O. Box 1577
Salisbury, MD 21801
Strawberry specialists. 30-page
catalog and planting guide lists over
30 varieties. Wholesale and retail.

48. Mayo Nurseries
Route 14
Lyons, NY 14489
Fruit specialists. 8-page catalog
includes many varieties of dwarf
and semidwarf apples. Wholesale
and retail.